An Authentic & Colourful Portrait of Days Gone By

Based on a 60-year-old manuscript that surfaced only recently, *The Rise of the Toronto Jewish Community* paints one of the most colourful and authentic portraits yet to emerge of what is now Canada's largest Jewish community, from its earliest days to about 1950, highlighting its strong immigrant and Yiddish flavour.

Here are vivid thumbnail sketches of many early synagogues, "anshei" congregations, landsmanschaft organizations and immigrant aid societies, along with a gallery of key personalities from the community's formative period. The author, himself a prominent figure in his day, brings Toronto's vanished Ward neighbourhood back to life with vivid descriptions of the soup kitchens, soda parlours, steamship agents, coffee houses and Christian missions that once graced its predominantly Jewish streets.

The narrative also offers detailed accounts of the evolution of the local Yiddish press, Jewish labour unions and indigenous garment industry on Spadina Avenue, as well as of the consequential garment workers' strike at the T. Eaton Company in 1912. The text is enhanced with many period photographs and illustrations, a glossary of Yiddish and Hebrew terms, and an afterword by the late Benjamin G. Kayfetz.

Shmuel Mayer Shapiro *was born in Mozir, Russia, in 1887, came to New York as a youth, and began to study to become a rabbi. Feeling increasingly drawn to socialism, he left the yeshiva and came to Toronto where he organized a pioneering branch of the cloakmakers' union. As a sideline he began writing at $2 a week and in 1912 became city editor of the* Yiddisher Zhurnal *or* Hebrew Journal, *Toronto's long-publishing but seldom profitable daily Yiddish newspaper; he eventually took it over as publisher and remained at its helm until 1957. Active in the Workmen's Circle and other Jewish organizations, he was a gifted orator who spoke at many community events and occasionally served as an arbitrator in labour disputes. He was also a provincial justice of the peace and an honourary president of the Canadian Jewish Congress. He died in Toronto in 1958.*

The Rise of the Toronto Jewish Community

Shmuel Mayer Shapiro

Toronto   2010

ISBN 978-0-9784435-2-8

THE RISE OF THE TORONTO JEWISH COMMUNITY. BY SHMUEL MAYER SHAPIRO. Copyright © 2010 by Now and Then Books. All rights reserved. No part of this publication may be reproduced in any form or by any means, electronic, mechanical or otherwise, except for brief passages quoted in the context of a critical review, without prior written permission from Now and Then Books.

The publisher would like to thank Mrs. Temi Rosenthal of Toronto for giving us permission to publish her father's manuscript. Thanks also to Mrs. Eva Kayfetz for allowing us to reprint her late husband Ben Kayfetz's essay on the Yiddish press.

The front cover shows a view of Spadina Avenue above College Street, looking south towards the lake in April 1957. The back cover shows the Goel Tzedec synagogue (top) in 1928; interior of an unidentified synagogue in the Spadina area, 1957; and a postcard image of the Holy Blossom Synagogue, Bond Street, ca 1910.

Library and Archives Canada Cataloguing in Publication Data

Shapiro, Shmuel Mayer, 1887-1958
    The rise of the Toronto Jewish community / Shmuel Shapiro.

Includes index.
ISBN 978-0-9784435-2-8

    1. Jews -- Ontario -- Toronto -- History. 2. Jews -- Ontario -- Toronto -- Societies, etc. --History. I. Title.

FC3097.9.J5S43 2010   971.3'541004924   C2010-900846-4

Contents

Author's Foreword (1950)   9

1   The Beginnings of Jewish Communal Life in Toronto   11
Talking Politics ~ Assisting the New Arrivals ~ The Christian Missionaries ~ First Kitchen for the Unemployed ~ Genesis of Local Organizations ~ Workmen's Circle 1908 ~

2   The Yiddish Press   39
The Yiddish Press in Toronto ~ Popular But Not Profitable ~ Bankruptcy — and a Succession of New Owners ~

3   The Shaping of Social Life in Toronto   55
Occupations & Trades of the Early Immigrants ~ Role of the Steamship Agents ~ The State of Jewish Education ~

4   Synagogues, Congregations & Rabbis   67
The First Reform Congregation ~ The Richmond Street Synagogue ~ The Bond Street Synagogue ~ The Holy Blossom Temple ~ The Rise of Landsmanschaft Organizations ~ Shomrei Shabbos & Rabbi Joseph Weinreb ~ Some Early Documents of Historical Interest ~ Machzikei Hadat ~ Goel Tzedec Congregation ~ Beth Hamidrash HaGadol Chevra Tehillim ~ Rabbi Jacob Gordon, z"l ~ The Rise of the "Anshei" Congregations ~ The Ostrovtzer Shul (Cecil Street) ~ Chevra Shas & Rabbi Abraham Price ~ The Kiever Congregation ~ The Polish Shul (Beth Yakov) ~ Hassidic Congregations ~ Shaw Street Shul (B'nei Yisroel) ~ The Yavneh Congregation ~ Beth Yehuda ~ Agudath Yisroel Anshei Sefarad (Palmerston Avenue) ~ Beach Hebrew Institute ~ Shaarei Shomayim Congregation ~ Beth Sholom Synagogue ~

Contents

5   Jews in the Needle Trades   111

Role of the Hebrew Journal ❧ Jewish Manufacturers & Unions Blaze the Trail ❧ The Cloak Trade ❧ From Tailor Shop to Professional ❧ The Cloakmakers Union ❧ The Neutral Chairman ❧ The Rise of Hitlerism ❧ Insights of a Leading Manufacturer ❧ Dresses, Sportswear, Children's Wear ❧ The Men's Wear Industry ❧ The Strike Against Eaton's, 1912 ❧ United Garment Workers Union, Local 83 ❧ The Amalgamated Union and Its Accomplishments ❧ The Fur Trade ❧ The Leather and Pocket Book Industry ❧

Afterword, By Ben Kayfetz   147
Recollections and Experiences of the Jewish Press in Toronto

Glossary   153

Photographs & Illustrations   156

A Note on the Text   159

Photo Credits   160

Index   161

Author's Foreword
(1950)

THE WRITERS OF CANADIAN Jewish history, the most outstanding of whom are Messrs. Arthur Daniel Hart, Benjamin G. Sacks, Louis Rosenberg and the late Abraham Rhinewine, succeeded to some extent in documenting the beginnings of Jewish colonization in Canada. In his brief studies Mr. Hart even attempted to give an account of the first Jew or Jews who set foot on Canadian soil in *The Jew in Canada* (1926) and Mr. Sacks did likewise in his more scholarly *History of the Jews in Canada*, the first volume of which appeared only recently. However debatable some of their biographical findings regarding the first Jewish settlers, these books are the first successful attempts at a history of early Jewish colonization in Canada.

Yet not one of these historians, in the course of his writings, has at any time devoted himself to describing the life of any of the numerous Jewish communities so rapidly springing up throughout Canada. It is our conviction that had such studies been available to these writers their task would have been much easier and their pictures of the early Canadian Jewish scene more rounded and real. For what is mainly lacking in their work is the record of the many small but human efforts that go into the building up of a complex community.

It is our consciousness of how rapidly the traces of the early history of our own community are disappearing that compels us now to search them out and record them. This, mainly, is our excuse for undertaking the onerous task of compiling, for the sake of both our readers and the future historian, a record of some of the remarkable events and curious happenings that transpired in the early days of the Toronto Jewish community and helped to shape its particular form. In presenting these facts we make no pretension to exhaustiveness; this work is not a full history of Toronto Jewry. Our aim is only to gather and preserve the known and forgotten facts about our early Toronto history and to keep that knowledge from being entirely lost.

Unfortunately there are but few manuscripts of historical interest and we have ferreted out only too few personal memoirs of any importance. At no time in the past was any thought given to the making and keeping of records. It was therefore necessary for us — if our labours were to be of any real benefit to the future historian — to examine carefully and authenticate each individual fact before accepting it. For most of our facts we had to rely on the recollections of those of the early Jewish settlers in Toronto whom we succeeded in interviewing; owing to the lack of written records there was no other means of corroboration. Carefully as we checked the information given us it must still be borne in mind that much of this personal testimony is without actual documentary proof.

However, having lived in Toronto continuously for the past forty-eight years and having been associated with the only local daily Jewish newspaper since its founding in 1912, we were privileged to witness the birth and development of the local community and we can personally attest to the reliability of much of the information presented here. As he is not attempting a formal history, the present writer feels no special need to arrange his material according to some fixed method. The most that he strives for is a chronological order in the presentation of the facts.

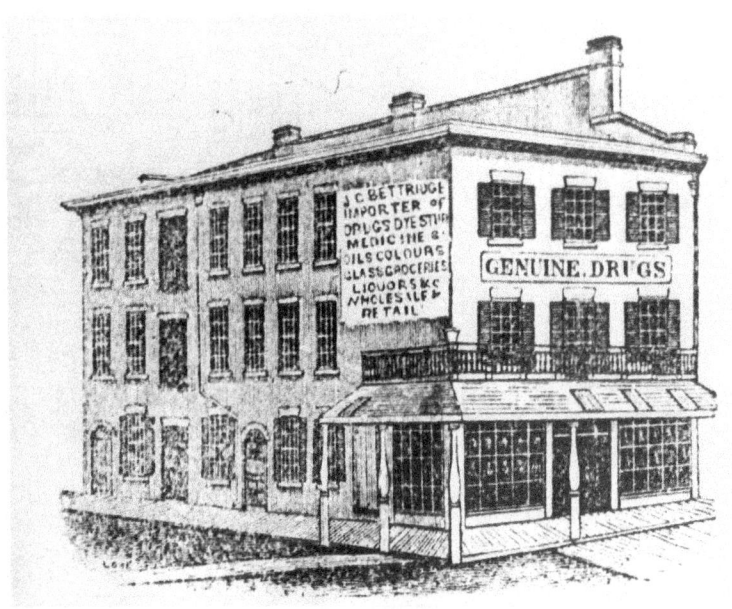

Site of Toronto's First Minyan

Members of Toronto Hebrew Congregation, also known as Holy Blossom, prayed in a third-floor room above Coomb's Drugstore, southeast corner of Richmond & Yonge, between 1856 and 1875. Entrance was by way of the middle door on Richmond Street.

1

The Beginnings of Jewish Communal Life in Toronto

THE STORY of the local Jewish community does not begin with the first Jew that settled in the then-small city that bore the Indian name of Toronto, meaning a trading post or rendezvous. There is some evidence of the presence of a few Jews in Toronto as early as 1817. We have examined the Toronto city directory for the year 1838 in which there occurs the Jewish-sounding name of Charles Goldsmith, Jeweller. But after careful investigation we have become convinced, despite the opinion of some Jewish writers,

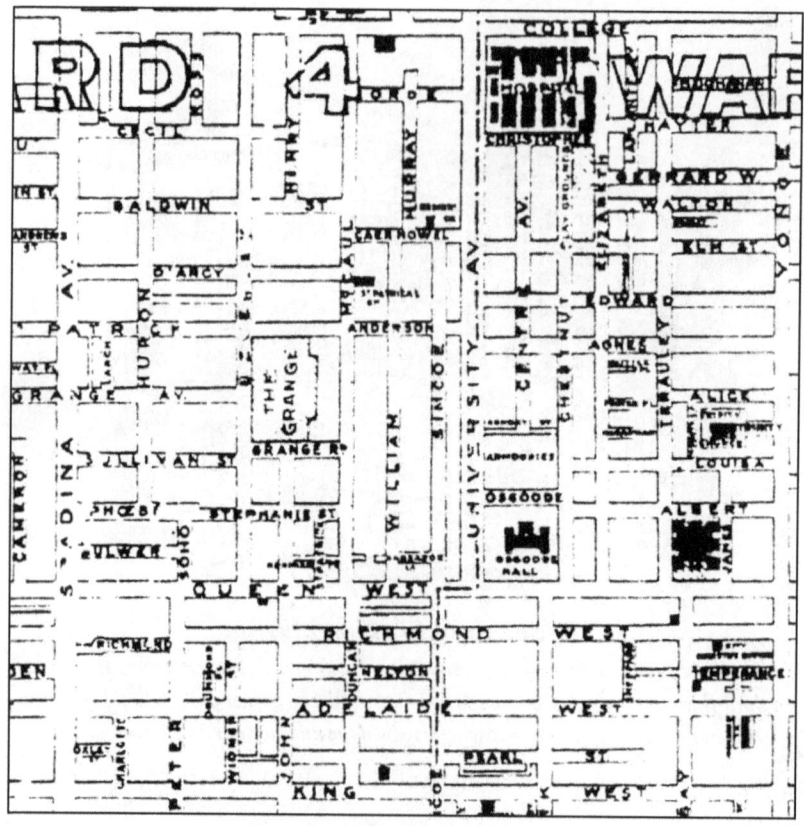

Section of Downtown Toronto, 1912
In the 1890s, most of Toronto's Jews resided in this central section of the city. Some also lived in the east end on streets like Sackville, Berkeley and Ontario.

that Mr. Goldsmith was in reality not a Jew but a Dutch Christian.

In 1852, however, we find the first evidence of organized activity among local Jews. A "Hebrew Benevolent Society" was formed with the aim of providing help for any indigent Jews that happened to reach the city. The group left no record behind of its activities but the society was officially registered with the provincial registrar of Ontario.

Another step towards some form of local organization was taken with the founding of the Holy Blossom Synagogue in 1856. A little later several small congregations, with services usually held in rented rooms, sprang up in the Jewish quarter of the city. But this form of organization was almost wholly religious in character, the social activities of the members having to do almost exclusively with affairs of the synagogue. However, as the local Jewish population grew in size, chiefly because of increased immigration from Eastern Europe, the situation slowly began to change. An important factor was the gradual movement to Toronto of Jewish settlers from the small towns and villages of Ontario. They came from Kingston, Hamilton, Niagara Falls, Chatham, even from as far north as North Bay. Cut off from the mainstream of Jewish life in Canada, leading a lonely isolated existence among Gentile neighbours, these people were naturally attracted to a rising Jewish centre. In their distant homes, they were concerned about the lack of opportunities for the education of their children, and anxious about the future of their young daughters, eligible suitors being distinctly lacking where they were living.

It was largely these older immigrants, who came dribbling into the city from the then-remote villages throughout the province, animated by the desire to find the intimate Jewish atmosphere they lacked at home, who first embarked on the task of organizing Toronto Jewish community life. To this group belonged such now well-known families as the Bennetts, the Allens, the Abramskys who came from Chatham; the Caplans who came from North Bay; and the Pullans who came from Ottawa. Moving to Toronto for a variety of reasons but chiefly because they hoped to lead a fuller Jewish life here, these families were foremost in leaving their stamp on the organized life of the city's Jewish community.

On the other hand, the immigrants newly arriving from Europe were for the most part too much absorbed in their own immediate problems to be much concerned with thoughts of organizing the community. Only the immigrant youth, who brought over to Canada the Zionist and socialist ideals they embraced while yet in the old country, showed a lively interest. Fairly large as the Jewish population of Toronto then was — almost 1500 in 1890 — it had no institutions of any kind apart from a few synagogues. There were no schools, no welfare organizations, no recreational societies. In short, there was no Jewish social life. What little there was, was confined to the family circle into which the stranger found it very difficult to penetrate.

At that time, in the early Nineties of the last century, the Jewish population of Toronto was concentrated in a small area bounded by Yonge Street on the east and McCaul Street on the west, and extending from Richmond Street on the south to College Street on the north. This same neighbourhood has today been largely taken over by Chinese and Negroes. In the Nineties, however, a street such as Simcoe was considered in somewhat the same light that "Forest Hill" is now. It was a wide tree-lined avenue with many spacious and attractive houses. The respectable, well-to-do Jew was glad to own a house on such residential streets as Centre Avenue, Agnes Street, Elizabeth Street, Edward Street or Walton Street. The poorer Jew, on the other hand, had to live in a shabbier neighbourhood — on York Street, for instance, or Foster Place or Louise, Teraulay, Albert, Chestnut or Armoury streets. The reader can better obtain a picture of the distribution of the Jewish population in Toronto at that time by examining the map we have reproduced on page 12.

A considerable number of Jews at that time resided in the east end of the city — the section east of Yonge Street, on Sackville Street, Ontario Street and Berkeley Street. A few Jewish families were to be found on Jarvis Street, then a fashionable Gentile residential street, as well as on several streets north of College and west of Yonge. The east-end Jews were mainly immigrants from England, Germany and Holland and certain districts in Galicia. These Jews held aloof from their East European co-religionists, contact only taking place when the former needed to buy kosher meat, Jewish baked bread, or *challah*, the traditional braided loaf eaten on the Sabbath day. The only tie between the German and the East European Jew was a philanthropic one — the German Jew providing financial assistance to the poor East European immigrant.

The *Yehudim*, the name by which the rich German Jews were popularly known, led a more or less assimilated life, very few of them remaining for long in the Jewish camp. The frequency of mixed marriages together with the numerous conversions that took place has practically wiped them out, so that few traces remain of these one-time Jewish families. None of the descendants of the early families of Nordheimer, King, Sutton, Harper, Lyons, Conan and Gould are today Jewish. Oddly enough, one can still see on some of the tombstones in the Pape Avenue Cemetery, the first Jewish cemetery in Toronto, the names of some of these early German Jews, together with engravings of prayer shawls and phylacteries, and inscriptions stating that the deceased was laid to rest in his religious vestments.

The foundations of an organized Jewish community life had already been laid by the time the present century was reached. The movement then slowly under way received a powerful impetus from events taking place in

A Restaurant in the Ward
The New York Kosher Dairy Restaurant, corner Albert and Elizabeth streets, 1912. The block was torn down that year to make way for the City Registry Office.

Russia such as the Russo-Japanese war. These events in a distant land had an immediate effect on the fate of the Toronto Jewish community. Suffering under a corrupt and despotic regime and fearing conscription into the Czar's armies, many young Russian Jews decided to emigrate. Canada had an immediate appeal for them. Some had already heard about the country from relatives overseas; others were willing to go to any place that offered a chance for a better life. Canada, to a good many, was a logical destination. The country was reputed to be a land of miraculous opportunities; its doors were wide open. There were no obstacles in the way of entry provided one's health was good.

The chief difficulty for these people was how to get out of Russia.

The borders of the Czarist empire were closely guarded and a Jew found illegally crossing was dealt with severely. By ingenious means, by paying large bribes to border officials and often by risking their lives in dangerous journeys across mountains and rivers, many managed to escape from the country. Of this group, a large number made their way to Canada, many of them to Toronto. The majority were single men. Most of those that were married came without their wives and children, either because they lacked passage money for them or because it was too dangerous to cross a border accompanied by one's family. A knowledge of these facts is important for a proper understanding of the background of these early immigrants.

Arriving in Toronto, the newcomers usually moved into neighbourhoods in which Jews were already established. They would rent rooms in the homes of relatives or residents hailing from the same home town. It is important to remember that a certain proportion of these immigrants did not come here with any intention of staying permanently. Some hoped to return to Russia as soon as the war with Japan was over. Owing to the uncertainty of their plans, and because their knowledge of the country's language and customs was nil, most of these people gratefully accepted any job available, enduring many physical hardships before finding something more suited to their natures.

The immigrants who arrived in Canada between 1903 and 1907 were for the most part a serious hard-working band, but there was also a small anti-social element among them. Ruffians in the old country, they continued in their old ways in the new land. Among them were a few habitual criminals, social misfits and chronically frustrated young men. There were also some married men, who, separated from their families overseas and eaten up with boredom and loneliness, turned to questionable and immoral pursuits. Small as this group was, the notoriety it gained soon caused considerable anxiety in the Jewish community.

In sharp contrast to these people was the intelligentsia, which arrived at the same time. Also small in number, it exerted nevertheless a most beneficent influence in the growing community, informing it with a living soul, so to say, and with dynamic vitality. The intelligentsia was divided into many groups, too many in fact, all more or less at loggerheads. There were Bundists and anarchists, moderate socialists and revolutionary socialists, Zionists and territorialists, Hebraists and Yiddishists. Each group tried to gain converts to its cause and to propagate its own special brand of social philosophy among the masses.

At first some of these groups wanted to unite with similar Canadian groups, but efforts in this direction were futile. There was too wide an ideological gulf between the native organizations and the immigrant ones. The ideas of the native Canadian socialists, for example, were not nearly so militant as those of the Jewish immigrants. As a result the Yiddish-speaking intelligentsia became increasingly isolated from its English opposite number. Separate Yiddish-speaking clubs and societies began to be formed. A socialist club was established at 185½ Queen Street West, a territorialist society at 72 Elm Street, a Zionist organization on Elm Street, and a cultural society open to everybody regardless of ideology on Simcoe Street and another one at 210 Elizabeth Street.

The first attempts at creating some form of community organization were made spontaneously — that is to say, without any conscious planning, without the promoters exactly knowing what they were doing. The groups mentioned above began to organize meetings and small social gatherings in private homes, on some special occasions even hiring a public hall for an affair. But although these public affairs frequently attracted large crowds, they cannot be said to have had as their aim the creation of community consciousness. Their chief purpose was rather to interest potential members in the ideology of the organizations sponsoring them. But these activities were the heralds of the larger community ventures that were to take place soon afterwards.

A stronger stimulus to the development of the community spirit came from the landsmanschaften. These were groups formed by immigrants coming from the same home town or from the same region. When Polish Jews, for instance, arrived in Canada, it was natural for them to seek out and mingle with others who had come from Poland. Lonely and bewildered, these Polish newcomers shared with the immigrants already here a common background: they had the same traditions and, above all, the same speech — important cementing factors for people beginning to take root in a land whose environment was new, whose customs strange, and whose language difficult. Thus it was that at first the composition of the landsmanschaften was based on national origin. There sprang up landsmanschaften of Polish Jews, of Russian Jews and of White Russian, Galician, Lithuanian and Roumanian Jews.

As the Jewish population of Toronto increased, it became easier

Newspaper Sketches of Peddlers in the Ward
At left, boys playing buttons, 1905. At right, a collector of rags and bottles, 1908.

for the newly-arrived immigrant to meet people who had come from the same district as himself. The next step therefore was the forming of landsmanschaften consisting of people from the same home town instead of from the same country. In quick succession there blossomed forth societies of former residents of large cities like Warsaw, Lemberg, Minsk and Wilno. Later came those of smaller places such as Ostrovtze, Kielce, Bobruisk and Bialystok. And lastly came landsmanschaften from small towns like Plotzk, Mozir and Kovne.

The chief task of the landsmanschaften was to keep alive among the immigrants the spirit and atmosphere of the old country. Furthermore, the landsmanschaften became a clearing house for information about the old home town, where most of the Toronto Jews still had relatives and friends. A landsman who wished to know what was happening in his old home only had to go to a meeting of his society — usually in the house of a neighbour — to find out the latest news. There was always sure to be someone there who had just come off the boat bursting with eagerness to tell what he knew. Landsleit would get together in the evening to talk about their families or friends still in Europe or to reminisce over a bottle of wine about childhood days in sleepy villages on the banks of the Vistula or the Dnieper.

When mail arrived from the old country the excitement was boundless.

Everybody would gather round the lucky person and make him read the letter out aloud. Privacy didn't exist for these landsleit — and for a very good reason: there was always the likelihood that there might be some mention of their own families in the letters their neighbours received. In a word, the landsmanschaften were for the lonely immigrant the letters he didn't get, the news he didn't himself receive, the warmth and intimacy he hadn't yet elsewhere found. Eventually the landsmanschaften evolved into *fareinen* — into sick benefit societies, welfare organizations and fraternal orders. But in the early days of their existence, they were the only friend the immigrant had. It was to them that he turned for help or comfort when his heart was heavy or his wallet empty. Little as it was, the assistance the landsmanschaften gave was sometimes all that stood between the immigrant and starvation, sickness, and sometimes even death.

Before 1900 the Jewish working class in Toronto was insignificant in size and influence. Poor as they were, the immigrants found it easier then to turn to middle-class pursuits such as peddling and retail selling for their livelihood. Small stores catering to the special needs of Jewish customers were opened in the now downtown area of the city. There were kosher butcher shops and bakery stores in which kosher dairy products could be attained. Many immigrants turned to peddling and retail selling. At first they did their business with fellow Jews but as their knowledge of English improved they ventured more and more into Gentile neighbourhoods, sometimes journeying to adjacent towns and villages to buy and sell.

The first Jewish bakery in Toronto was opened by Mr. Rubin on York Street, the first Jewish butcher shop by Mr. M. Cohen on the same street. Mr. Mordechai Dickman was the first local *shoichet* (ritual slaughterer of kosher meat) joined the same year by a second, Rabbi Isaac Halpern. The first junk shops were started by Mr. Mendel Granatstein and Mr. Leo Frankel; shortly afterwards Mr. Shloime Godfrey, Mr. Moishe Siegel and a number of others went into the same business. Most of the employees in these junk shops were pious Jews who refused to take any jobs where it was necessary to work on the Sabbath. Consequently, they were sometimes shamelessly exploited by callous employers. They were forced to work in the shops Saturday evenings when the Sabbath was over, sometimes very late into the night. Occasionally they had to work on Sundays — behind locked doors, of course — in order to make enough to live on.

Beginning in 1903 the number of skilled workers arriving here from the old country steadily increased, and continued to do so until the First World War began and all immigration stopped. It was hard enough for the unskilled worker to find a place in Canadian industry. It was even harder for the skilled worker. In the first place he couldn't speak English well enough to explain his qualifications to his employer, or, if he found a job, to discuss his problems with the Gentile worker at his side. Canadian industrial methods were, moreover, radically different from those in Europe. The immigrant plumber, electrician or locksmith who had learned his trade in Europe quickly discovered that his previous experience was not enough. He needed to know more about new tools and machines; and it wasn't easy to find a place where he could apprentice.

Consequently, very few immigrants found jobs in the trades they had worked at in the old country. Metal workers, furniture designers, blacksmiths and shoemakers alike had to turn to new trades. The shoemaker in the old country, for example, had had to sew and stitch each pair of shoes by hand. In the Canadian shoe factory this was no longer necessary. There were machines for sewing the work cheaper and faster. Only the old-country tailor proved somehow able to continue at his old trade, and even his opportunities were not particularly bright. Consequently, we repeat, most immigrants abandoned their old trades to search for new ones. In the ensuing scramble the old-country blacksmith turned presser, the shoemaker became an operator at cloaks, and the locksmith turned to selling old clothes. With few exceptions, too, most of these workers didn't remain long at their new occupations but changed them frequently, until at last they found ones that suited them.

Much to their dismay, the immigrant workers discovered that there was no labour movement to speak of in the city. What unions there were, were weak: the leadership was conservative and generally speaking, the rank and file lacked political consciousness. For the Jewish worker this was a surprising state of affairs. At home, in Europe, he had grown accustomed to the constant struggle between workers and employers. He had helped organize unions, had taken part in strikes, had stood on the picket line distributing strike literature. No wonder then that he couldn't stomach the lethargy of the native-born factory workers and turned to organizing unions of his own. It is this factor that explains the rapid rise of small Jewish unions for each trade, or branch of a trade, and their feverish political activity.

Talking Politics

In the first decade of the present century, from 1900 to 1910, the Jewish population of Toronto showed very little interest in politics. The city of Toronto, like the rest of the province, was solidly Conservative. Despite some opposition from the Liberals, the Conservative candidates were always elected to office with overwhelming majorities. There was no socialist party to vote for and the workers seldom put forward a candidate of their own. The more well-to-do Jews, the assimilated *Yehudim*, and the parvenu rich invariably backed the Conservatives. Sometimes, when an issue affecting the interest of the local Jewish population as a whole would arise, a few of these individuals would step forward, unbidden, as representatives of the community. In time these self-appointed Jewish leaders became the recognized intermediaries between the civic administration and the Jewish community. They were befriended by politicians seeking office and utilized as vote getters. In return for political favours these so-called leaders of the community would promise to get the Jewish vote for their candidate. On his side the candidate, in his campaign speeches, would promise to defend the interests of his Jewish constituents if elected to office.

Apart from these professional Jews, however, few other Jews took an active interest in politics, whether municipal, provincial or national. They saw little real difference between the two parties or their candidates. One was as good or as bad as the other and in any case, they felt that both parties represented the same interests. Furthermore, the immigrant couldn't understand the English speeches of the rival candidates, the issues were obscure to him, and there was no Jewish candidate running who could appeal to this national pride. In the eyes of the immigrant all parties were alike in that they took very little interest in the affairs of the working man.

The centre of the immigrants' political activity, forty and fifty years ago, was to be found in the numerous ice-cream parlours and Jewish soft drink pubs that had sprung up, like mushrooms after a rain, all through the Jewish district. As soon as the immigrant managed to accumulate a few dollars he would invest his saving in an ice-cream parlour. The sale of ice cream was actually only a very small fraction of the storekeepers' business. Here it was possible to get a meat sandwich or a hot cup of tea, a package of cigarettes or a glass of siphon water, the popular drink at the time (today's bottled drinks were still unknown). In the back of

Day of Atonement, 1910
*Dressed in their synagogue finery, Jewish residents of the Ward
walk past an ice cream parlour on the fast day of Yom Kippur.*

the store were a few small tables where the customers could sit down and order a meal. However, most of the time the regular customers just sat and talked, or read the newspapers, or played a game of dominos or cards. The discussions were always lively and often stormy, with everyone in the store taking part. Jewish problems were carefully analysed; political affairs were discussed noisily with no pretense of objectivity. Tempers often flared and it was not uncommon to have an argument end in a brawl. Young suitors courted their belles under the benevolent eyes of the storekeeper and his customers. Not a few happy marriages had their beginnings in these ice-cream parlours.

A few of these places were frequented exclusively by the local Jewish intelligentsia. After work, intellectuals of every type, Zionists and socialists, *genossen* and *chaverim* (beneficiaries and comrades) would drop in for a cup of tea or a game of chess, often staying long into the night, talking and arguing, with everyone trying to prove the superiority of his group or ideology.

One of the most popular places stood at the corner of Louisa and Elizabeth Streets, in the very heart of the then Jewish neighbourhood. It was owned by several partners, Mr. Shimon Colofsky and the two brothers Messrs. Samuel and Joseph Rosenfeld. There are good grounds for believing that their chief reason for opening the store was to provide a social centre for immigrant intellectuals. Themselves workers — the two Rosenfelds made a comfortable living as carpenters and Mr. Colofsky ran a small business with some success — the owners were eager to promote the intellectual life of the young community. When their day's work was done, these gentlemen liked to repair to their store, wait on the customers, and listen to the various discussions going on. Some evenings the customers were entertained with more formal discussions, readings from the Yiddish classics and talks on Zionism, territorialism and other subjects of special Jewish interest.

But literature and politics were not the sole interest of the habitués. Chess was very popular and tournaments were held frequently. One of the most interesting players was a Mr. I. Rosen, a bookkeeper by trade. He was always the first to come and the last to leave, and was looked up to as a great authority on all matters relating to chess. He spent all his time at the chessboard, only occasionally absenting himself to take some little job that he couldn't very well refuse.

Another such store, belonging to Messrs. Chanan and Boris Dworkin, was located at the corner of Albert and Chestnut Streets. It was later moved to 64 Elizabeth Street. The proprietors extended credit to their regular customers and their generosity soon brought them a larger trade. The customers coming here were, generally speaking, bitter opponents of Jewish nationalism, being mainly Bundists, anarchists and other anti-Zionists.

A third store, located at 102 Agnes (today's Dundas) Street was owned by Mr. Yitzhak Herman, a native of Wolin. The store was a favourite rendezvous for Poalei Zionists, Talmudic students who liked a game of chess, and various young men starved for the life of the mind. Passing for an intellectual, Mr. Herman was in reality a rather naïve person. Watching the customers queuing up to his counter for cigarettes and tobacco, he decided that the retail tobacco business had a great future. When he learnt further that the Imperial Tobacco Company made huge profits buying tobacco and making their own cigarettes, he decided that there was no earthly reason why he couldn't do the same thing. He began to package and sell his own tobacco a few cents cheaper per package and watched with elation as sales rose briskly. He soon became inebriated with visions of getting rich quick. Unfortunately, a week after he launched his scheme he was visited by revenue officers from the Excise and Revenue branch of the Dominion government. Mr. Herman now discovered to his dismay that the violation of patent rights was a serious matter and the evasion of excise duties even more so. Mr. Herman had a hard time convincing the authorities of the innocence of his scheme. The legal suit cost him a tidy sum but he was lucky to escape with his whole skin. Previous to this incident, he had worked in a local shoe factory; now he was forced to return to his old job and leave the management of the store to his wife.

A fourth ice cream parlour was opened at the corner of Armoury and Chestnut Streets by a Mr. Greisman. Most of Mr. Greisman's customers were Galician Jews who had come from the part of Poland annexed from Austria after the First World War.

Another ice cream parlour, Michaelson's at 97 Agnes Street, became the headquarters of Roumanian Jews and the meeting place of young men and women with a passion for the theatre. Having acted on the stage in the old country, Mr. Michaelson, the owner of the store, never stopped talking of his past theatrical glories. He was always nostalgically reminiscing of the good old days when his appearance on the boards was the signal for tremendous applause. Vanity apart, however, Mr. Michaelson's interest in the theatre was sincere. He was in fact the first in Toronto to produce a Yiddish play. In 1904 he organized an amateur theatrical group with himself as director. And a year later, in 1905, he was instrumental along with Mr. Abramov in bringing to Toronto a cast of professional actors from New York, thereby laying the groundwork for the legitimate Jewish theatre which later arose in the city. The company gave a series of performances of famous Yiddish classics in a hall that Michaelson rented for the occasion. But interest on the part of the community was lukewarm and the group had to disband after a few months.

Two of Toronto's first Jewish restaurants opened in 1900 or slightly thereafter. One, at 119 Elizabeth Street, was run by Mrs. Tucker; the other, on Teraulay Street, was managed by Mr. M. Goldenberg. These restaurants had their regular customers who used to stay on after meals to talk with friends. But these restaurants never equaled in popularity the less pretentious ice cream parlours as centres for social gatherings. In fact, apart from the few synagogues and a small socialist club on Queen Street, there was no Jewish centre at all for people to meet and spend an evening together in a friendly atmosphere. The situation didn't improve until two Toronto Jews — Mr. S. Fleishman, a local musician, and Mr. David Sussman, one of the founders of the Ostrovtzer Synagogue — realizing the needs of the growing Jewish population of the city, opened the Center Palace Hall on Elm Street.

Assisting the New Arrivals

In the early years of the century, the small Jewish community of Toronto had many serious problems to cope with. The most pressing one was, of course, how to absorb the large number of immigrants that were steadily arriving. The housing situation in the city was serious. Accommodation for the newcomers had to be found at once, and food, and clothes. The vast majority of the arrivals were wretchedly poor, with their worldly possessions literally on their backs, in the form of heavy bundles strapped onto their bodies. Their tattered suitcases bulged with hand-sewn pillowcases, feather-filled bedding, heavy woolen underclothes, and the traditional pair of silver candlesticks. They had no money to speak of. Their clothes were old and worn, their bellies empty, their spirits low.

There was then no Canadian Jewish Congress or Hebrew Immigrant Aid Society to turn to. These and similar organizations did not arise until later. In those days the small Jewish community in Toronto had no organizations to look after the needs of the immigrant. There were no experienced social workers to meet the immigrant as he came off the boat, to provide him with a lodging however temporary, and to advise him on the choice of an occupation. The immigrant then had to rely on his own resources, initiative and enterprise.

Nevertheless, the newcomers did receive some assistance, however small, from the generation of immigrants before them. This help was largely private and voluntary. And it did not come from the rich who, generally speaking, held themselves aloof from the Yiddish-speaking masses.

Shocked by the general apathy towards the plight of the new arrivals, a number of the more humanitarian members of the community decided to do something. They personally began canvassing for funds, knocking at doors

Landmarks of the Early Community, ca 1912
Top photo is believed to be Center Palace Dance Hall. Centre left, McCaul Street Synagogue; centre right, Lyric (National) Yiddish Theatre. Bottom, the Polisher Shul, B'nai Jacob, before its move to Henry Street. From a Christian missionary booklet.

of private houses and asking for donations of money, clothes or medicines. They would then hand over the money or articles of clothing to the most needy cases — sometimes keeping a family from starvation, sometimes saving a sick child, sometimes helping an expectant mother with medical care she couldn't herself afford. This help was sometimes considerable and was deeply appreciated by the newcomers. A few unscrupulous persons sometimes took advantage of the wave of public sympathy for the suffering immigrants and exploited this sympathy for their own profit: callously they appropriated the moneys they collected.

More organized attempts were also made to collect relief to alleviate the widespread poverty within the Jewish population. Although such efforts met with only slight success, they were nevertheless the first organized activities in the young community. A single instance will suffice. A small dispensary was opened at 218 Simcoe Street and free medicine distributed to the needy. In the same three-storey house there was also an orphanage, taking up two rooms. One of these rooms was used as a *cheder*, where the children were given an elementary Jewish education; the other was reserved for the staff, which consisted of one supervisor. The house had originally been rented at $25 a month and was eventually bought for $11,000. When, six months after the building was purchased, the first payment fell due — the amount was exactly $50 — there wasn't enough money on hand. Fortunately, an employee of the Chestnut Street branch of the Crown Bank, Mr. Joseph Gurofsky, offered to provide the money if he were given a promissory note signed by several respectable men. Ten persons came forward to endorse the note, each guaranteeing to pay $5 if it was not redeemed. Mr. Gurofsky then gave the money and the interest on the house was paid. When the note was finally redeemed it was given to Mr. S. Frimes, a local jeweller, in whose keeping it has since remained.

ᛞ *The Christian Missionaries*

Again, there were those who tried to profit from the misery of the immigrants; this time, however, there was no attempt to fleece the public and the motives were spiritual, not financial. We are of course referring to the missionary societies, whose purpose was to save souls — Jewish souls. And particularly those of the unhappy immigrants who could at times barely manage to keep body and soul together. These missionary groups were quick to take note of the often desperate plight of the newcomers and proceeded to intensify their work among the Yiddish-speaking masses. Converted Jews, able to speak Yiddish, were sent out to preach the gospel of Christ to their erring brethren and to bring the "light" to them. Of course, material help was offered too. Mission houses and hostels, where hungry and homeless newcomers could get a meal or a night's lodging, were built in the Jewish district. And the missionaries at the beginning had, it must be admitted, some success. Many an immigrant, hungry and without a roof over his head, was forced sometimes to take advantage of their material offers. There were no Jewish institutions at the time to care for the hungry and the unemployed.

The first of the Jewish missionaries in Toronto was Mr. Henry (Nachum) Singer. He had come here from Leeds, England, and was placed in charge of a mission on Centre Avenue, in the heart of the Jewish quarter. He had two female assistants, both very devout Christians. Singer himself was no scholar and his speech was a mixture of German and Yiddish. He stood over six feet tall and possessed a powerful physique, a very impressive figure indeed. His voice was deep and magnetic and when he preached in the street he could easily be heard a block or two away. Every morning a few Jews, hungry and out of work, would turn up at his mission. After the services, which consisted of short prayers and some hymn singing, they would be served coffee and bread. Then Mr. Singer would set out, accompanied by his visitors of the day, on a round of visits to the local factories to try to find them work. And often he was quite successful, managing to find jobs for at least a few of them. The others, still without work, would return with Mr. Singer to the mission where they would again be served bread and coffee, sweetened by a sermon on brotherly love.

On almost any summer evening one could find Mr. Singer standing on some street corner in the Jewish quarter surrounded by members of his mission and preaching to the Jewish passersby. After the group hymn-singing that was customary on such occasions, Mr. Singer would step forward to deliver his familiar exhortation. In no time at all a large crowd — and usually a few hecklers — would gather round him and listen smilingly to his florid oratory. It was his habit to introduce his sermon with a Hebrew text from the Old Testament. He would begin in a low voice, point out the divine authority of the particular verse he had chosen, then try to prove that the Jewish prophets had foretold the advent of the Christ. Full of deep emotion, his voice would slowly rise in volume, until at the climax of his sermon it would be reverberating all through the neighbourhood. The sermon finished, Mr. Singer would invite his listeners to accompany him to the mission, there to enjoy a light repast.

As far as is known Mr. Singer made only three converts during his long ministry in Toronto and in the eyes of the Jewish community these did not represent a great loss. The first of the converts was a local cloak operator, Mr. Sam Brown by name, who had been born in Bialystok and had lived in Leeds, England, before coming to Canada. His reputation in the community was not very high and it was alleged that he spent most of his time loafing on street corners. The second was a somewhat "queer" individual, Mr. Hershel Solomon, about whose origin nothing was known. The third of Mr. Singer's converts was Mr. Yankel Braverman, who had come here from Zhitomir, Poland, where he had left behind a wife and children. It was believed Mr. Braverman changed his faith in order to marry a Gentile woman that he had fallen in love with. All in all Mr. Singer was not able to make much capital out of his successes in the Jewish community. Despite police protection — there were always two constables present at these meetings to keep order — none of the converts dared to preach or take part in public hymn singing in their old neighbourhood.

Another mission house, much larger than the first — it occupied a new three-storey building — was located at 257 Elizabeth Street, at the corner of Elm. It was headed by the Rev. Sabati B. Rohold, a converted Jew born in Jerusalem. As a young man Rev. Rohold had gone to England to study. He had been converted there to Christianity and had entered a Protestant theological seminary, eventually graduating as a minister. At the mission house on Elizabeth Street Rev. Rohold was in charge, with Mr. Singer and Mr. Henry Bregman under him. When a Jewish convert was to be baptized, Rev. Rohold would always personally officiate at the ceremony. He was a man of wide learning, familiar with the Talmud and other Jewish religious works. Quite often he would challenge one of the Toronto Orthodox rabbis to meet him in a public debate. Needless to say, his humiliating challenges were never taken up. Knowing from experience the futility of debating over religion, and regarding it as beneath their dignity to accept, the rabbis ignored his challenges. All in all the worthy

Christian Missionary in the Ward, 1912
A former Jew, the Rev. Henry Singer (left) proselytized on downtown street corners, attempting to convert Jews. His successes were few.

reverend made very little headway among the Toronto Jews.

Mr. Bregman, a third Jewish missionary to preach in Toronto, was born in Homel, Russia. Before coming to Canada he had lived for some time in England, where he was converted. Mr. Bregman had had a rigorously religious upbringing and in his youth had married the daughter of an Orthodox rabbi. Indeed, for a short time he had preached in the Northampton and Vine Court synagogues in London, substituting for the Skidler Maggid, the regular preacher. We learnt something of Mr. Bregman's history from Mr. Joshua Singer, one of the oldest members of the staff of the Toronto *Hebrew Journal*. Mr. Singer had been a writer for the *Jewish Express*, a Yiddish weekly published in London, England at the turn of the century, and in the course of his duties had got to know Mr. Bregman quite well. When he met him again years later in Toronto, Mr. Singer was astonished to learn that Mr. Bregman had become a missionary. When he demanded an explanation, Mr. Bregman confided that he had tried in vain to obtain a divorce from his wife, a singularly ugly woman, and that because he couldn't bear to live with her any longer, he had out of spite and in order to force her to part from him, turned to Christianity, in which in the end he perhaps found a sincere consolation.

The missions were of course more interested in the immigrants' spiritual salvation than in their material welfare, but converts were more easily made when material assistance was given. The Jewish apostates considered the immigrants very fair game; conditions were favourable. The country was passing through a severe crisis: unemployment was widespread, jobs hard to get. Many newcomers experienced actual hunger, frequently not knowing where the next meal was coming from. There were no Jewish organizations to turn to for assistance. In their despair, some of the immigrants came for help to the missionaries. A free meal was always available; occasionally a job. Indeed, in the eyes of some, the missionaries were not an unmitigated evil. After all, they helped materially and it was believed that few Jews would actually be lured from their faith. Some of the Gentile manufacturers were more apt to take on Jewish workers if they were recommended by the missionaries. Generally speaking, the Jewish population could do very little for the unemployed. Only Rabbi Solomon Jacobs, then at the head of the Holy Blossom Synagogue, took an active interest in their plight and tried to help. As a rule, however, the unemployed immigrant had to shift for himself.

Scott Mission, Spadina Avenue, 1949
*Founded 1908 by Rev. S. B. Rohold, its first home was at Elm & Elizabeth.
Another ex-Jewish missionary, Morris Zeidman, relocated the Mission
briefly to Bay Street, then to Spadina Avenue.*

First Kitchen for the Unemployed

From 1905 to 1907 Canada was in the grip of an economic crisis. The Jewish population was especially hard hit. The majority had lived in Canada for only a short time and were bewildered by the turn events had taken. They had come here hoping to find work, and opportunities, and security; now many of them were thrown out of employment, jobs were scarce, and their savings were gone. Some roamed the streets, hungry, weary and penniless. Anxious to alleviate their distress, a number of public-spirited working people — a few tailors, carpenters and small businessmen — got together and organized an emergency kitchen to look after the feeding of the unemployed. A large house on Teraulay [*Bay*] Street was leased for this purpose by Mr. David Levine. The rent was $6 a month. Shortly afterwards, in the beginning of 1906, the first Jewish public kitchen in Toronto was officially opened.

Furniture, dinnerware, kitchen utensils and cutlery came from a variety of sources. The Shomrei Shabbos Synagogue on Chestnut Street

Letterhead of Toronto Jewish Kitchen, 1932

donated wooden benches. Tables were donated by the Kiever landsleit, many of whom were second-hand furniture dealers. Messrs. Hershel Wilder, Benzion Nussbaum and S. Weber supplied the glassware and cutlery. Carpenters and painters donated their labour, repairing furniture, washing floors and painting walls. A few people volunteered as waiters and dishwashers. Mrs. Tucker and Mrs. Solway, two prominent Toronto ladies, undertook to look after the cooking. Meals were served twice daily, at noontime and in the evening. Because of the scarcity of dishes it became necessary to serve the unemployed in groups of twenty-five.

Most of the money for maintaining the kitchen came from the poor; the more well to do ignored the undertaking. The money was raised by public subscription, the majority of subscribers paying five cents. Several subscription lists we examined showed the highest individual contributions to have been fifty cents. Many donations were in the form of gifts of food. The following items appear in a typical list:

"2 loaves of bread (a single loaf cost 4¢, a double loaf 7¢)
"¼ bag of potatoes (a bag cost 12½¢)
"2 lbs of onions (cost 5¢)."

The regular collectors were Cantor Maurice Caplan and Mr. Moishe Caplan, a pants presser. The latter devoted most of his time and energy to his voluntarily assumed task. A few of the leading workers were Mr. Joseph Layefsky, Mr. Abraham Layefsky, Mr. M. Blechman, Mr. L. Tredler and Mr. Maurice Langbord.

There were some, however, who though hungry and without money to buy food were reluctant nevertheless to come to the kitchen. Ashamed in the first place of having to accept public assistance, they regarded it as a further humiliation to have to eat their charity meals before the eyes of strangers. In deference to their feelings an innovation was made in the manner of distributing relief. The author of this innovation was a garment worker, Mr. Leibish Finkelstein, who thought up a way of overcoming their reluctance. At his suggestion it was decided to prepare box lunches containing sandwiches, soup and meat, to be distributed once each day to needy persons calling for it.

After a short time the kitchen had to close owing both to lack of funds and lack of experienced personnel. A second attempt to run a kitchen was made a year later. This time the chief sponsors were businessmen and insurance agents. A large run-down house was leased and a hostel added to provide free lodgings; but, though money was more abundant this time, it too had to close down, and it was not reopened until three years later, in 1911.

⤳ Genesis of Other Local Organizations

The first two sick benefit societies in Toronto were founded by Polish and Russian immigrants about 1905. These were the Mozirer Sick Benefit Society, which was organized in the home of a Mozirer landsman, Mr. Bregman, and the Pride of Israel Sick Benefit Society, today the largest organization of its kind in Toronto. The years between 1905 and 1914, when the First World War broke out, were for the Jewish community of Toronto a period of phenomenal growth. The Jewish population grew by leaps and bounds, and the Jewish residential quarter became more and more congested and began spilling over into neighbouring Gentile districts. Slowly Jews began moving away from Elizabeth, Edward, Chestnut, Elm, Centre Avenue and Simcoe

Streets, making their way as far west as Spadina and as far north as Bloor.

Jews became more conspicuous in retail business, in real estate, and in manufacturing. They began taking a greater interest in civic affairs, in provincial matters, and in national politics. With a generation of Canadian-born English-speaking youngsters growing up, steps were now taken to organize an educational system to keep children who were receiving all their education in the Toronto public schools from becoming alienated from their Yiddish-speaking parents. Labour came of age; the unions grew strong enough to let their voice be heard occasionally in community affairs. The American Jewish press — chiefly of course the New York Yiddish dailies — extended its influence over readers of Yiddish.

Cultural activity became more pronounced. Intellectual leaders of American Jewry were invited to Toronto to lecture on Yiddish topics and drew large audiences. Some of those who spoke here were Abraham Cahan, B. Feigenbaum, Morris Rosenfeld, Joseph Barondes, Sholom Aleichem, Dr. Chaim Zhitlowsky, Yitzhak Isaac Hurwitz, Yehoash and Emma Goldman. For a while Toronto figured as the main centre of Canadian Jewish cultural life. European celebrities came here to give lectures. One of the first to visit Toronto was Dr. Nachman Syrkin, the founder of Labour Zionism, who was at that time working on plans for a Jewish parliament.

Simultaneously there emerged a native literary movement. Under the leadership of such local intellectuals as Messrs. M. Gar, S. M. Shapiro, Samuel Rosenfeld, Yitzhak Herman, M. Babitch, Noah Steinberg and Melech Grafstein, cultural activities quickened. Special literary evenings were arranged, lectures frequently held. There were public readings from the works of the Yiddish classics, public debates and forums. However, it was not always easy to draw crowds to hear a lecture. Sometimes indeed it took a lot of prodding to get any kind of a turnout. The brilliant Nietzschean scholar, Noah Steinberg, for instance, had to advertise his own lectures. He used to print circulars at his own expense and personally distribute them from house to house in the Yiddish district. Unable to make money from his writings, he made his way by working as a tailor in a local factory.

In 1907 a number of Jewish socialists formed a Young Socialist Club with Mr. S. Zalkin as first president. A Labour Zionist Club was organized by Mr. S. M. Shapiro, Mr. Sam Berezovsky, Mr. M. Gelfand and Mr. Moishe Dan. Interest in the Yiddish theatre grew, with a number of local amateur groups springing up.

Teachers of the National Radical School, 1911

The Jewish National Radical School of Toronto was a secular institution under the guidance of labour leader Isaac Matenko and writer Abraham Rhinewine. After a few years it modified its radical spirit and became known as the Workmen's Circle Peretz School. Rhinewine, standing at left, was editor of the Hebrew Journal in the 1920s.

➢ Workmen's Circle, 1908

Branch 220 of the Workmen's Circle was founded in 1908 with seventeen members; Mr. M. Skurko was the first president. To qualify for membership, an applicant had to pass a medical examination. Two of the Circle's original members were Mr. L. Tredler, who ran a cleaning and pressing shop, and Mr. Sam Fasser, a machinist by trade. In a souvenir programme published on the 10th anniversary of the branch, there appears the following from the hand of Mr. L. Tredler: "The first Toronto branch of the Workmen's Circle was founded on September 18th, 1908."

Before 1904 there had been no public place where radicals could get together for an evening's talk. Organizations like the Hebrew Benevolent Society were much too conservative for them and their programs intellectually unsatisfying. If one of the radicals happened to drop in to the Zionist Club on Beverley Street — where there was always a *Tageblatt*, a copy of *Minkes' Yom Tov Bletter*, or perhaps a somewhat risqué novel to read — with a copy of the socialist *Forverts* under his arm, he was likely to find himself tossed out on his ear. Indeed, most of the time radicals lived a rather isolated life in the young community.

The first attempt to organize the radicals, by founding a branch of the Workmen's Circle in Toronto, was made by a few individuals of advanced opinions, notably Mr. M. Eiges, Mr. Sol Rivkin and Mr. L. Sapirstein. Sixty persons registered and paid their full initiation dues. But because of legal difficulties encountered, the attempt failed. A second try made in 1906 proved equally abortive. Out of frustration, some individuals joined the Russian Socialist group, the Jewish section of the Socialist Labour Party, and the Socialist Territorialist Society. Others, less politically minded, joined the newly-formed Pride of Israel and Mozirer societies.

In August 1908 Mr. Chana Dworkin and Mr. Abraham Epstein approached the writer of this article for the purpose of discussing the formation of Workmen's Circle branches in Canada, with particular attention to be paid to Toronto. Mr. Abraham Epstein himself was a former president of the Workmen's Circle in the United States. After thoroughly discussing the matter we decided to approach the local Jewish socialist club to ask them to help us to organize the branch and to perhaps become its nucleus. We requested permission to address the club and received an invitation to do so at one of its regular meetings. When we got there we discovered, to our dismay, that our request was not on the evening's agenda.

The idea of disbanding in order to transform themselves into an organization primarily concerned with encouraging unionism and promoting sick benefit societies — rather than with seeking to spread socialism — was apparently repugnant to the executive of the Jewish branch of the "Socialist Party of Canada." They seemed to consider our suggestion impertinent and unworthy of serious attention. Nevertheless, when the meeting ended the chairman rapped his gavel on the table and announced that Mr. Abraham Epstein, a visitor from New York, together with a committee representing the Workmen's Circle, wished to address the meeting. He added that out of courtesy he was letting us speak but that our subject was of little interest to the members.

Mr. Epstein was visibly annoyed by the chairman's attitude but he somehow managed to control his anger. He said it was necessary to have a Workmen's Circle movement in Toronto and that it was proper — nay, obligatory — for socialists to back such an organization. When he finished the matter was briefly debated by the members and it was finally decided that they — that is, the socialists — would sponsor the new organization but that for the time being they would remain "members at large" only. After this meeting the campaign for members was begun in earnest. Fully two-thirds of the initial applicants came from the socialists (among them were three women). The rest came from the local anarchist group, the socialist labour party, and the socialist territorialist society.

Of the original eighteen applicants, seventeen were accepted at once as members. All but one had successfully passed the medical examination required by the constitution. Then, on September 18, 1908, Branch 220 of the Workmen's Circle was officially declared into existence. It was these seventeen pioneers who laid the foundation of the present great Workmen's Circle organization in Toronto. Out of this branch there eventually sprang the socialist territorialist branch of the Workmen's Circle, the socialist labour branch, and the anarchist branch. On the first anniversary of the founding of Branch 220, a Literary Evening and Peanut Banquet was held for members and their friends. Though the membership was then only sixty, more than 1,000 people attended. It was at this banquet that the Independent Cloakmakers Union, one of the strongest pillars of the International Ladies Garment Workers Union, was first organized.

Pioneers of the Toronto Cloakmakers Union, 1911

Early Staff Photo, Hebrew Journal
S. M. Shapiro and Abraham Rhinewine are seated at left in this undated photo. Seated at right is Joshua Singer with Messrs. Cohen and Friedland standing behind him.

2

The Yiddish Press

IT IS BEYOND QUESTION that in Toronto in the early days of the century, nearly all immigrant opinion on the social questions of the day bore the label "Made in the USA." This is not said facetiously, nor is it put forward as a proof that some subtle form of American imperialism was at work. No, it is the literal truth. For it is a plain fact that Canadian Jewish opinion was then to a very great extent formed and shaped by the Yiddish dailies published in the United States. The New York Yiddish press monopolized the Canadian market. It had no rivals

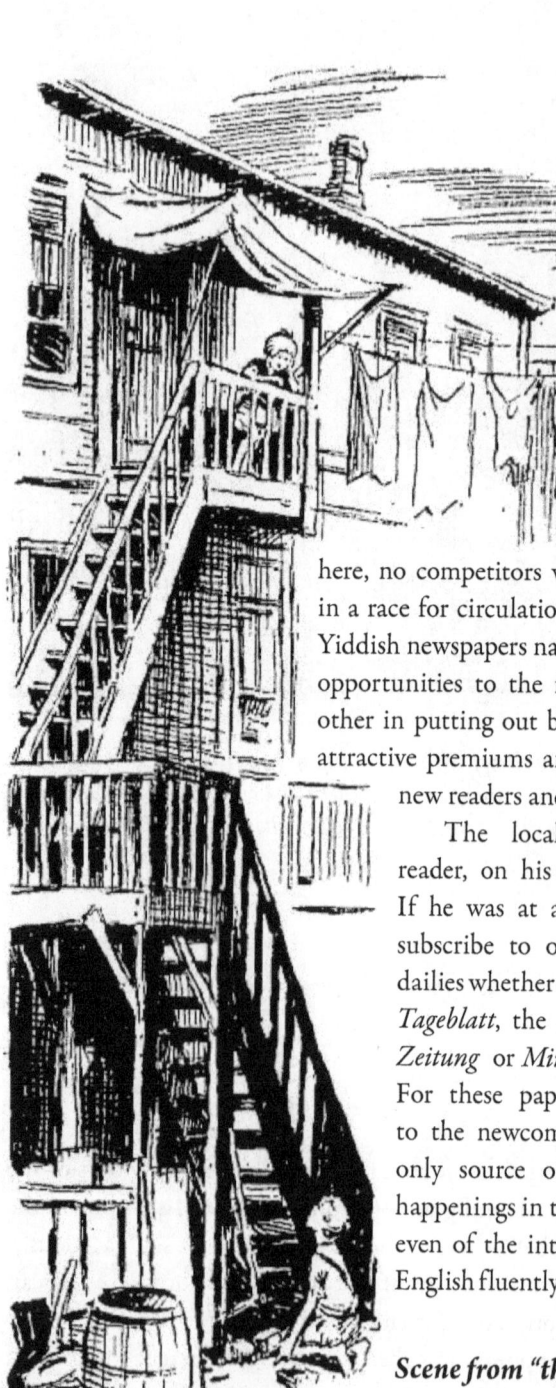

here, no competitors with whom to engage in a race for circulation. And the American Yiddish newspapers naturally exploited their opportunities to the full, vying with each other in putting out bait — in the form of attractive premiums and prizes — to catch new readers and new subscribers.

The local Jewish newspaper reader, on his side, had no choice. If he was at all literate he had to subscribe to one of the American dailies whether it was the *Forverts*, the *Tageblatt*, the *Wahrheit*, the *Abend Zeitung* or *Minkes' Yom Tov Blatter*. For these papers were a necessity to the newcomer, being almost his only source of information about happenings in the outside world. Few even of the intelligentsia could read English fluently enough to go through

Scene from "the Ward," 1920
Certain scenes in the Ward seemed reminiscent of the Lower East Side.

the local English dailies. Consequently they were forced either to read the American Yiddish papers or none at all. The fact that the New York papers seldom arrived punctually, quite often appearing two or even three days late, bothered the readers very little. For them the news was always fresh.

The frenzied period of mass migration, the greatest in modern Jewish history, was faithfully mirrored in the Manhattan Yiddish dailies. One couldn't read through a single number without absorbing something of the smells, sights and sounds of New York's crowded East Side. The rich spectacle of immigrant life, its turbulence, its drama, was always being presented to the gaze of the readers. And like the spectacle itself, Yiddish journalism was lusty and robust and colourful. The front pages of the Yiddish newspapers bore a startling resemblance to the tabloids of a later period. They were sensational, devoted to the seamier side of life. Stories of crime and lust were splashed across the front pages. Headlines screamed the latest outrages against society. Special reporters were assigned to cover particularly heinous crimes, in order to thrill readers with eye-witness accounts of the details. Sob sisters, using up many columns of print and thousands of words, would play up the sordid drama for all it was worth, pulling at the reader's heartstrings and catering to his hunger for scandal. The victim's family life, the testimony of witnesses, the noise and confusion in the courtroom, the behaviour of the accused, the conduct of the jury — all the various details were juicily dished up for the delectation of the reader.

But while the front page was obsessed with the violent and sensational side of life — the side of life guaranteed to thrill the reader — the remainder of the paper was given over to more serious matters. There were dozens of articles written by the leading Jewish writers of the day on the most diverse subjects, history and literature, philosophy and science, economics and politics. Although heavy at times, the articles were never dull and pedestrian. They were meant for the masses, not for a highbrow minority. The aim of the writers was to raise the cultural level of the immigrants, teach them the social facts of life and equip them for the social struggles lying ahead. The style of Yiddish writing was vigorous, forceful. There was none of that dull anonymity, that impersonal coldness that characterizes press association material and syndicated articles today. The writers were vehement, sometimes even vituperative. Columnists of rival newspapers attacked each other mercilessly; they pelted each other with every abusive word in the dictionary. What they lacked in manners

Cartoon from a New York Yiddish Weekly, 1910
A butcher assures a Jewish woman that his shop is kosher, despite visible evidence of "treif" everywhere. From Der Groiser Kundes ("The Big Prankster"), a satirical weekly.

they made up in gusto, and the readers lapped it all up, begging for more.

The Toronto Jewish reader, like his relative on East Broadway, was fascinated by the antics of his mentors. A murder on Lexington Avenue sent a shudder down his spine as he sat at his bench in some dingy factory on Spadina Avenue. He held his breath as he read what the murderer ordered for his final meal before beginning his death march to the electric chair. On the more serious side he became completely absorbed in the feuds constantly going on between writers of opposing papers. If he was a subscriber to the *Tageblatt*, a paper standing for religious orthodoxy, he would be horrified at his neighbour reading an article by Feigenbaum in the *Forverts*, the bible of the Jewish socialists, in which the latter inveighed against God and religion. If he was an adherent of the Jewish Socialist

Bund, which preached that the Jewish working class could prosper only under a socialist system and that Jewish nationalism was a reactionary aim, he would grow choleric at the sight of a friend reading the *Tageblatt* or another Zionist daily that preached mass settlement in Palestine as a solution to the Jewish problem. If he was not interested in politics, the reader was more than likely to take sides in the literary controversy that for years engaged the energies of Abraham Cahan, editor of the *Forverts*, and Louis Miller, editor of the *Wahrheit*.

Readers seldom transferred their allegiance to another paper. Of course, occasionally, when a radical became wealthy he might swear off reading the *Forverts* and turn to the *Tageblatt*, the pillar of conservatism. But a reader's loyalty to the paper of his choosing was usually everlasting unless some revolutionary event caused him to change his views. The influence of the American Yiddish press at that time cannot indeed be overestimated. It left its stamp on a whole generation of immigrants in Toronto as well as elsewhere. For the Toronto Jew the New York press had only one shortcoming: it had no local news, no local writers to give the columns a local flavour. It was quite natural therefore that Torontonians nurtured on American Yiddish newspapers should want to emulate the kind of life they saw mirrored in their pages. Their political views, their social ideals, were an exact copy of those held by New York Jews. The Workmen's Circle, the National Workers' Alliance, the Cloakmakers' Union and similar organizations founded here were American not only in origin but also in the spirit and pattern of their development.

✈ *The Yiddish Press in Toronto*

Before 1912 there were no regularly published Yiddish newspapers in Toronto. True, in 1910 two brothers — their family name was Simon — came here from New York and started an Anglo-Jewish weekly, the *Toronto Wochenblatt*. But the paper did not appear regularly and was a financial failure. In less than a year it ceased publication altogether. A similar fate overtook another Yiddish weekly, *The Press*, which was started a year later by two Toronto Jews named Moses and Levy. The first successful attempt to publish a local Yiddish newspaper was not made until a year later, in 1912. Near the end of that year, Mr. H. M. Hirsch, a young Russian Jew born in 1880 in Yekaterinoslav, near Kiev, arrived in Toronto. The Jewish

A Yiddish Print Shop, 113 Elizabeth Street, ca 1911
Owner Pesach Edell (left) with staff at the Royal Printing Company, which printed material in Yiddish and Hebrew. The shop is at far left in the 1930s-era photo below.

press in Toronto can be said to have begun with his arrival.

Mr. Hirsch's coming here was the result of a chance meeting that took place in the Canadian border city of Windsor. While there on a visit from Detroit, where he was living, Mr. Hirsch happened to meet Rabbi Meir Zvi Levy of Toronto, who was also visiting Windsor. The meeting proved to be a fruitful one for the Toronto Jewish community. Rabbi Levy took an instant liking to the young man and pressed him to come to Toronto to live, even promising to find him a job with a businessman he knew. Acting on the rabbi's suggestion, Mr. Hirsch moved to Toronto and was soon engaged as a bookkeeper by Mr. Joseph Pomerantz, owner of a dry goods business on York Street.

Little is known about the early life of Mr. Hirsch, who was very reticent about his private life. He was, most of the time, a quiet, rather shy man who shunned the limelight. His aversion to publicity was such that he never allowed himself to be photographed in public. Once launched on an undertaking, however, he would devote all his energies to bringing it off. At such times his enthusiasm for his work would be contagious, inspiring everybody around him. Mr. Hirsch was an exceptionally able and talented journalist and when after being here for a short time he discovered that there were no Yiddish newspapers published in Toronto he was amazed beyond words. He promptly decided to remedy the situation and in December 1912 began publishing a weekly newspaper, the *Yiddisher Zhurnal*, commonly referred to in English as the *Hebrew Journal*. A little later, heartened by a wide public response, he decided to publish the paper as a daily. In January 1913 the first copy of the daily edition of the *Hebrew Journal* appeared on the newsstands. Its appearance marked an epoch in Toronto Jewish journalism and from that day to this the *Hebrew Journal* has been a flourishing and influential institution.

Mr. Hirsch succeeded in interesting a trio of Toronto printers — Messrs. Goldberg, Moses, and Rabinovich — in his project. Both Mr. Goldberg and Mr. Moses had come from Roumania and were experienced typesetters, owning a small commercial printing business at Queen and York. The third man, Mr. Abram Rabinovich, operated a small printing shop on Hagerman Street near Elizabeth. Impressed by Mr. Hirsch's arguments, and seeing prospects for a profitable new enterprise, the two printing establishments decided to pool resources and launch into the publishing field. As it was absolutely necessary to have a linotypist, they hired Mr. Joshua Singer, a man born in Lechwitz, White Russia, who had, before coming to Toronto, lived for some years in England where he had been a Hebrew teacher.

The weekly edition of the *Hebrew Journal* was never a financial success. It carried too few paid advertisements. But its moral influence was extraordinary. Every Friday morning — the day on which it appeared on the streets — crowds would gather in front of the office, scrambling to get a copy before the issue was exhausted. The price of the paper was a cent. People were starved for local news; the majority couldn't read the English papers. As a result the paper would no sooner appear on the newsstands than it would be grabbed up by a hungry public.

But the revenue from circulation was hardly enough to cover printing costs. There could be no talk of wages for editor and contributors. The publishers themselves did all the mechanical work of typesetting and printing without deriving a cent of profit from their investment. Indeed the only one to receive wages — and they were small indeed — was Joshua Singer, the linotype operator, without whose services the paper could not have got along. Had it not been for the industry and character of the editor, Mr. Hirsch, and the hope of the publishers that the paper would ultimately pay its way, this weekly, like the others before it, would most certainly have folded.

Apart from his work as a linotype operator Mr. Singer also wrote articles for the paper under the pen name of Achizevel. The main task of looking after the paper fell on Mr. Hirsch's shoulders, however: he had to gather the news himself, compose the leading articles, proofread the material and, in addition, handle the circulation, the advertising and all the other details connected the proper functioning of a newspaper. If it is remembered, moreover, that he did all this while continuing to hold down his bookkeeping job, then his accomplishment becomes all the more remarkable. It was indeed fortunate for his publishers that Mr. Hirsch was a man of prodigious energy and a fluent and prolific writer who could work for twenty hours a day without letting up.

➲ Popular But Not Profitable

The *Hebrew Journal* had been on sale for only a few months when it began to attract the attention of the intelligentsia. Several young men with an interest in journalism offered to become contributors. One of the first was Mr. Shmuel M. Shapiro, the writer of the present book, who was the secretary of the United Garment Workers Union. The job he took on was that of writing the daily feuilleton. Another was Mr. Archie B. Bennett, at that time still a student at Queen's University. From his student days right down to the present time Mr. Bennett has always taken an active interest in the affairs of the Jewish community. His early Yiddish articles in the *Journal* created a stir in the community, their substance and their style both clearly heralding the appearance of a fresh and important talent on the Jewish scene. Mr. Bennett turned his great journalistic gifts to the service of the community, writing honestly and fearlessly on the burning issue of the day, at the same time raising with his criticism the cultural standards of the Jewish population of Toronto. Throughout his career Mr. Bennett had held steadily to one objective — the democratization of Jewish life.

The weekly itself was interesting, full of colour and very readable. It covered every phase of Jewish activity that might be of interest to its readers. The rich and bustling immigrant life of that time was mirrored in its lively news columns and articles. Special prominence was given to important local happenings, to community organizations, and to all kinds of social activity. As editor, Mr. Hirsch, believed that in order to succeed he must print any material of wide reader interest. He therefore concentrated on human interest stories about local figures. These were always written with warmth, often with sympathy and understanding. Though gossipy at times, these stories never violated the standards of good taste.

The response was instantaneous and overwhelming. Here, at last, the public found what it could never get from the American Yiddish newspapers. Circulation jumped at once, in a short time reaching 4,000 — an extraordinary figure — and it kept climbing steadily. Gratified by the warm public response, but recognizing that the weekly's revenue from circulation was far short of the money needed to run the paper at a profit, Mr. Hirsch began to take steps to change it over to a daily.

His first step was to organize a new publishing house, the Hebrew Publishing Company of Canada, headed by himself, Mr. S. Goldberg and Mr. Abram Rabinovich. Stock in the company was offered to the public at $10 a share, and the owners were soon deluged with requests from ordinary working people who wanted to become shareholders in a Yiddish newspaper. A fourth partner now came into the business, Mr. Abraham Sher, an insurance agent connected with the Metropolitan Insurance

Company. Carefully, dollar by dollar, Mr. Sher saved his money until he had accumulated a bank account of $2,000. Then he decided to invest it all in a business. The *Hebrew Journal* seemed to be going places and Mr. Sher told himself that if he got into the business now there was a good possibility that he would be having a steady income from the paper as well as a share of the larger profits in the future. He was made general manager and put in charge of the advertising and circulation departments. In return for the $2,000 he put into the newspaper, Mr. Sher was given a share in the business plus 25% commission on the advertising he sold.

With the money received from Mr. Sher and from the sale of shares to the public a down-payment was made on a second linotype machine — the company already possessed one — and on a duplex printing press for ten pages. The machines, bought from the Canada Linotype Company and from Manton Brothers, cost a total of $25,000. After the machines were acquired new difficulties arose. The old building on Queen Street was not large enough for the machinery and then there was not another linotype operator in the city able to operate a Yiddish linotype machine. The first difficulty was solved in a hurry. Mr. Moishe Siegal, a Galician immigrant who owned a rag shop on Elizabeth Street, offered to lease part of the building he owned to the Hebrew Publishing Company. The second difficulty, however, was less easy to overcome. There were no Yiddish linotypists at all in either Toronto or Montreal. The only place where one could find one was the United States.

Fortunately this too was solved — purely by chance. The late Yehoash, one of the great Yiddish poets in America, happened to be visiting friends in Toronto in the fall of 1912. When he learned the trouble the owners of the *Journal* were having getting a linotype operator, he made up his mind to find one for them or bust. He was successful, and in the beginning of 1913 Mr. A. Lappiner, a Yiddish linotypist who had been working for the Hebrew Publishing Company of New York, was hired at $35 a week. Although the wages he was offered here were higher than those he was getting in New York, it is our opinion that Mr. Lappiner's only reason for coming to Toronto was to please Mr. Yehoash. Mr. Lappiner was an agreeable young man, eager to help with anything. He didn't stay in Toronto very long though, but before he returned to New York he managed to teach two other young printers the mystery of operating a Yiddish linotype machine.

Next, the editorial staff was enlarged. Rabbi V. I. Greenstein, now living in Los Angeles, was hired as assistant editor; the late Mr. Abraham Rhinewine, who had come from Poland as a young man and worked in an embroidery factory, was appointed news editor; Mr. I. Rosen, the chess expert mentioned earlier, was taken on as bookkeeper; and Mr. S. M. Shapiro was reporter, feature writer and feuilletonist all at the same time. Shortly afterwards another member was added to the staff. This was Mr. Moishe Dickstein, associated today with the Crown Life Company in Montreal. These five men made up the permanent editorial staff of the *Hebrew Journal* and were placed on a regular salary. (Actually, regular salaries were paid for only six weeks.) There were also others, not on the payroll, who contributed articles, stories and news features without getting paid for them. The most prominent of the contributors were Mr. A. B. Bennett, Mr. L. Rosenberg and Mr. A. Pact.

The appearance of the *Hebrew Journal* was an important step forward in the development of the local Jewish community as it put an immediate end to the chaos reigning in the community's affairs. The birth of the paper meant that at long last the Jews in Toronto were going to have an authoritative voice — an organ to express their views and analyse their needs. The immigrant would now be able to thresh out his problems publicly and at the same time learn something of the manners and customs of his adopted country. The Jewish worker and his union, the Jewish manufacturer and his association, the Jewish teacher and his school board — all alike would now be able to seek and obtain a sympathetic hearing. Every Jewish institution and organization, every society and club, was now assured of the widest publicity for its programs and activities. Indeed, the continued existence of the paper was vitally important to the community — a guarantee against a return to chaotic conditions.

Nevertheless the support it at first received was rather less than overwhelming. Indeed, instead of growing, the revenue steadily dropped. There never seemed to be enough on hand to meet the weekly payroll and bills kept falling due with monotonous regularity. Payments constantly had to be made on the machinery; paper, ink, stationery and other office supplies had to be purchased; gas, hydro and telephone service maintained. Yet for two years the paper somehow managed to stay afloat. The publishers struggled valiantly to meet their obligations, often borrowing money from private individuals anxious to support a Yiddish newspaper in the community. Each day it took a mighty effort on the part of owners and staff to get the *Journal* out in time. Several Jewish politicians active in the Conservative party bought up the majority stock in the paper. But when they discovered how much capital was needed to keep the paper going they quickly repented of their action and financially retired from the scene.

⇒ *Bankruptcy — and a Succession of New Owners*

In the end, in February 1915, the publishers went bankrupt. They lost everything they owned. Most of the equipment was offered for sale at a public auction. The printing press, the linotype machines, the duplex presses went for a song to Mr. Harry Wineberg, a local jeweller. Born in Lithuania, Mr. Wineberg had lived for some years in the United States before coming to Toronto. He knew nothing about publishing and his only reason for buying the machinery was that the auctioneer's price seemed a steal. "It originally cost me a mere few hundred dollars to buy the business," Mr. Wineberg later said. "Then I had to fork over another $15,000 to protect my original investment."

Mr. Wineberg tried to carry on from where the previous owners had left off. He kept the name of the paper and retained the staff both in the printing and editorial departments. However, he moved the presses from Mr. Sigal's rag shop to his own premises at 251 Queen Street West. Then, several months later, on May 15, 1915, Mr. Hirsch handed in his resignation as editor. At the same time Mr. Goldberg, Mr. Rabinovich and Mr. Abraham Sher, the original founders of the Hebrew Publishing Company, withdrew from the business. Mr. Rhinewine replaced Mr. Hirsch as editor-in-chief, Mr. S. M. Shapiro was promoted to news editor, and the job of reporter and feature writer went to Mr. H. Shmerler.

Sensing his shortcoming as a publisher, Mr. Wineberg began to hire outsiders to manage the business for him. One such was Mr. Saunders, who came from Ottawa. But Mr. Wineberg was invariably disappointed with the efforts of those he hired. Finally he decided to let some of the employees of the *Hebrew Journal* come into the business on a partnership basis. Mr. Wineberg felt that as partners they would be likely to take better care of the business, keep costs down to a minimum, and perhaps eventually put the paper on its feet. Acting on this hunch, Mr. Wineberg approached several of the employees. Naturally they jumped at the offer, grateful for

Hebrew Journal, Staff & Partners, ca 1920s
Max Clavir sits front row centre and Nathan Friedland is beside him with arms folded. Shmuel M. Shapiro and Abraham Rhinewine stand second and third from left.

the opportunity to turn businessmen. Thus four more partners were added to the business in 1919. The new partners were Mr. Abraham Rhinewine, the editor of the paper, Mr. Nathan Friedland, the linotypist, Mr. H. Shmerler, the feature writer, and Mr. H. M. Kirshenbaum, since 1915 the circulation manager. Mr. Kirshenbaum was also at different times society editor, humour editor and writer of serials.

Before qualifying for full partnership, however, each employee had to invest $2,000. Those that could not raise the amount were allowed to pay off the balance through weekly deductions from their salaries. After these contracts were signed Mr. Wineberg obtained an additional $21,000 by taking out a chattel mortgage on the plant's equipment. It was agreed that after the mortgage was paid off all partners would share equally in the profits. One year later, however, one of the partners dropped out. This was Mr. H. Shmerler, who decided to move to the United States. The others all remained as owners of the firm.

In 1927 Mr. Wineberg's interest in the paper was bought out for $25,000 by Captain Fred Johnson. A Gentile, Captain Johnson was a prominent supporter of the Liberal party who hoped to use the paper to advance his political fortunes. He intended to stand for election as candidate in the Jewish ward and believed that his connection with the Yiddish paper would stand him in good stead. Captain Johnson himself did not play an active role in the management of the *Hebrew Journal*. Instead he appointed as his agent Mr. Max Clavir, a prominent Jewish merchant originally from Roumania and then North Bay.

The firm now moved its plant and offices into a large building at 542 Dundas Street West which it rented from Mr. C. Sussman. The building has since remained the home of the *Hebrew Journal*. But Captain Johnson never realized his plans. It wasn't long before he became involved in a series of rather shady undertakings and lost not only his wealth but his reputation as well, eventually, as a matter of fact, landing himself in jail. The paper into which he had sunk nearly $45,000 couldn't survive this disaster and once again went into bankruptcy. In March 1931 the *Hebrew Journal* was put up for sale by the creditors and sold for $24,000 to a group consisting of Mrs. Etta (Lyon) Phillips, the wife of Alderman Nathan Phillips, KC; Mr. Nathan Friedland, and Mr. S. M. Shapiro. Mr. Friedland was placed in charge of the mechanical department of the paper and Mr. Shapiro became editor and business manager. Mr. A. Rhinewine and Mr. H. M. Kirshenbaum left the *Journal* and launched a Yiddish weekly, the *Tribune*. When this paper failed to make any progress, Messrs. Rhinewine and Kirshenbaum joined with Mr. Max Clavir in putting out another Yiddish newspaper, the *Jewish World*. But this paper too survived for only a short time.

The new owners of the *Hebrew Journal* organized a limited company, The Journal Publications of Toronto Limited, which they managed themselves until 1936. That year the company fell into arrears in rent and the owners decided that the proprietor of the building, Mr. David Sussman, should be made a partner as compensation for the money coming to him. This arrangement lasted until 1938, when the business was voluntarily handed over to Mr. Sussman, again for rent due. Mr. Sussman and Mr. Shapiro together managed the paper until 1940, when Mr. Shapiro largely through the backing of friends, was able to purchase the *Hebrew Journal* outright. He has since been its publisher and editor.

Mr. Shapiro's financial backers have expressly asked not to be mentioned by name. Their one desire was to make it possible for a Yiddish paper to exist in Toronto. When they made their investment they realized that the paper had little chance of making money. Indeed they made their investment in the full knowledge that what they put in would very likely never be taken out again. But they were filled by a profound need to serve the Jewish community.

We cannot conclude this brief history of the *Hebrew Journal* without mentioning a few of the men whose assistance in the past has made the paper possible. Among the editorial staff were the following:

A. Almi (Dr. B. Gitlin), 1917–19;
L. M. Benjamin, a noted barrister in Montreal, 1925–27;
Moishe Fogel of Montreal and Toronto, 1931– ;
Yitzhak Fogelman of Montreal and Toronto, 1925–31;
M. Z. Frank of Toronto and New York, 1938–39;
Rabbi H. Goodman of Toronto, 1944– ;
P. Halpern, 1920–25;
Lou Hayman of Toronto, 1943–44;
Kalman Hurwich of Winnipeg and Toronto, 1933– ;
A. M. Mandelbaum, later with the New York *Freiheit*, 1920–25;
Israel Rabinovitch, now editor of the *Canadian Eagle*, 1920–21; and
David Rome, of Vancouver, Toronto and Montreal, 1940–43.

Messrs. Frank, Rome, Hayman and Goodman were engaged full time in looking after the English section of the paper. Part-time employees on the English page included Mr. A. Abrams, now living in New York; and Mr. Ben Lappin, present executive director of the Canadian Jewish Congress in Toronto. There were also a number of temporarily employed editorial members in the Yiddish department of the *Hebrew Journal*. The most outstanding were:

Mendel Ackerman, poet and short story writer of New York, 1930;
David Apotov of New York;
Berl Baum, a talented short story writer of Wilkes-Barre, Penn., 1930;
Dr. S. Margoshes, executive director of the Zionist organization of Ontario in 1922 and 1923, now editor of *The Day* in New York;
N. Shemen of Toronto, 1930;
Meyer Weisgal of New York and Israel, ca 1930s.

The permanent members of the mechanical staff were:

Z. Abramovitz from 1948 on;

E. Akiba, linotypist, 1927 to 1932;
Sam Bayefsky, linotypist, from 1932 on;
Velvel Cohen, the only Yiddish duplex pressman in Toronto, 1915 to 1938;
Louis Flich, typesetter, 1925 to 1930;
Gordon Kosnetaz, typesetter, 1917 to 1925;
Harry Leventhal, typesetter, 1914 to 1920;
Adolph Wantroff from 1925 on; and
Louis Zelenko, linotypist, now living in Los Angeles, 1919 to 1926.

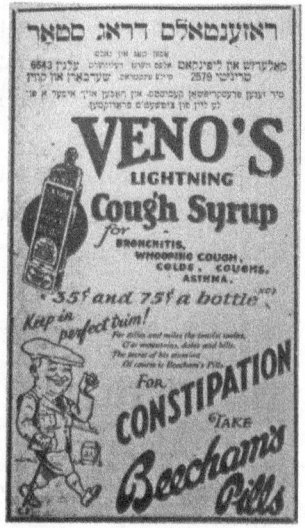

Ads from the Hebrew Journal
Top, Rosenthal's Drug Stores (two locations); centre, Folksverein Purim Campaign; and bottom, Rotstein Furniture Company's 14th anniversary sale. All from 1928.

Street Scene in Toronto's "Jewish Quarter"
Reproduced from Christian missionary pamphlet, 1912.

🎕 3 🎕

The Shaping of Social Life in Toronto

SINCE THE BIRTH of the *Hebrew Journal* as a daily newspaper, the tempo of social life among the Jewish population both in the city and in the scattered communities of the province has quickened and its quality has become, with the years, enormously richer. What is interesting and important is that whereas the influences shaping immigrant life were until recently almost wholly European in origin and character, now a new spirit deriving its sustenance chiefly from Canadian soil manifests itself in the community. Before analysing this

Mastheads of Five Yiddish Publications
From top: Daily Forverts (began publishing in New York, 1897); Kanader Adler (Montreal, 1907); The Hammer (Montreal, ca 1917); Daily Hebrew Journal (Toronto, 1912); The Mazik (Toronto, 1920).

new spirit we shall first call to mind some of the early influences.

The greatest, of course, as well as the most important, was the New York Yiddish press. The large dailies — the *Forverts*, the *Wahrheit*, the *Tageblatt* and the *Morgen Zhurnal* — together with the plethora of partisan periodicals published by the multitudinous political groups in New York, comprised the only source of news available to the Yiddish-speaking immigrant in Toronto. From them he received his cultural nourishment; they were his only contact with the outside world — the old world he had just left behind and the new one being created on the American continent. He wanted to know what was happening in Warsaw and Wilno and Kiev — it was only a few weeks, months or years since these cities had been his home — and he was happy to discover that the American Yiddish papers carried exhaustive reports on these places by its foreign correspondents.

Naturally he looked forward with great eagerness each morning to getting his paper, and he devoured it hungrily from cover to cover. Furthermore, the Yiddish press brought him an added pleasure, parading before his curious eyes as it did the colourful pageant of life in the teeming metropolis of New York, where many of his relatives and friends had gone after leaving home. In time the Jew on Spadina Avenue or College Street became more familiar with life on East Broadway and Orchard Street than with life in Toronto. This situation, alas, had unfortunate consequences. For while the American Yiddish press gave its Canadian readers a good helping of intellectual nourishment — it published short stories, essays, political articles, all of a high calibre — it completely ignored the background of the Canadian Jews. The attention of the American Yiddish press was fixed on the old country and on the American scene. The Jew in Toronto had no opportunity of learning about his new home, its social ways, its politics, its economics.

The second important influence was that wielded by the various political parties and groups. These were the Socialist Party, the Socialist Labour Party, the Socialist Territorialists, the Labour Zionist party (Poalei Zion) and the various anarchist societies. These groups likewise took little interest in Canadian affairs, completely neglecting the need of the immigrant to become integrated into the life of the new country. They were chiefly concerned with spreading among the Jewish workers of Toronto the ideologies they had brought from the old country. The programs and methods remained what they had been in Europe. Mentally they still lived in the Czarist empire, shouting revolutionary slogans that were more suited to conditions in backward Russia than to conditions here. At first the propaganda of these groups fell on fertile soil, for most immigrants arriving in Canada were familiar with oppressive conditions in Eastern Europe. The shouted slogans of the Bund, the Social Democrats, and the various revolutionary parties in Russia, Poland and Roumania still reverberated in their ears. But after they lived here for a short time the unreality of the social philosophies of many of these groups became apparent to them, and many began drifting away. It was from these groups, however, that the local intelligentsia was largely recruited.

Third in influence was the group consisting of the German, English and Western European Jews (including a few parvenu rich from Eastern Europe) who had settled in Toronto in the 1880s and 1890s. Although relatively small in number, this group had an influence far beyond its numerical strength. Without any real bonds with the majority of Eastern European Yiddish-talking Jews, from whom they often stood aloof, they nevertheless became their spokesmen — self-appointed, of course. From the ranks of these English-speaking Jews came the philanthropists, the social leaders, the British patriots. They set the tone in the Jewish community, telling the immigrant how to behave in public so as not to antagonize his Gentile neighbour, urging the Jewish worker to accept uncomplainingly whatever wages were offered, lest the employer should brand him as a troublemaker, preaching a philosophy of assimilation on the one hand and demanding obsequiousness towards the Gentile on the other. It was largely through these elements that the Gentiles had their first contacts with the Jewish immigrant. Another group that had some influence was that comprising a heterogeneous assortment of ambitious functionaries, social climbers and officious ward heelers who infested the community. Interested solely in advancing their own ends, these people often took it upon themselves to advise and guide the community.

These, then, were the main influences at work in the Toronto Jewish community during the early stages of its evolution. They could scarcely be called constructive forces, having resulted in little of lasting value to the community; sometimes, indeed, they even hampered its normal development. Most of the groups we have here discussed were less interested in the welfare of the community as a whole than in the promotion of their own ends, whether these were party interests or personal ambitions. The idea of the community as an entity was furthest from their thoughts — if it entered their thoughts at all. The only people who consciously worked to realize the ideal of a community were the simple folk — the ordinary working man, the small businessman, the housewife. It was largely on their initiative and through their labours that many of the important institutions of the community came into being. In later years certain so-called philanthropists tried to claim credit for the founding of this or that institution. But the truth is that not only did they not help to build these institutions, they very often fought tooth and nail against them, saying that they would be superfluous and an unnecessary burden on the populace. This was so in the case of the Old Folk's Home, the Jewish Hospital, the Jewish schools, the Yiddish theatre and similar institutions. The real founders were the poorer people, not the wealthy.

Occupations & Trades of the Early Immigrants

In order better to understand the difficulties involved in creating community institutions it is important to know something of the economic conditions of these early immigrants and of their occupations and trades. The Jewish population fell into several distinct levels. First there were the factory workers — the pressers, the operators, the cutters at cloaks and suits. Then came the people who worked for themselves and were their own masters: the buyers of old clothes who went from house to house in the Gentile districts, offering to pay cash for discarded or worn clothing; the rag peddlers who often went out in pairs with horse and wagon, buying up old clothes, rags, paper, broken kitchen utensils and other household goods; the pushcart peddlers who pushed their wooden barrows along the city's streets and lanes, shouting their traditional "rags and bones," often to the accompaniment of jeers or stones from unsympathetic bystanders amused by their outlandish appearance and speech.

After them came the dry-goods peddlers, dragging heavy bags crammed full of a wide variety of merchandise ranging all the way from shirt buttons to plush curtains, which they tried to sell to the housewives for cash or on the installment plan. There were also the so-called "bakers" — men owning their own horse and wagon who would buy a day's supply of bread from some small Jewish bakery which they would try to sell at a small profit to the neighbourhood grocery store or the individual housewife. Then came the people with trades — the plumbers, the carpenters, the shoemakers, the blacksmiths, the house painters. Usually these also worked on their own, sometimes starting out on their day's work with a small toolbox under their arm or occasionally having their customers come to their place of business, perhaps a small shed leased in the rear of a building.

Then there were the small merchants, who usually rented a small store and lived in crowded and dingy quarters overhead. These were the butchers, the grocers, the poultry peddlers, the tobacconists and the ice cream parlour keepers. And lastly there were the better-off commission agents — the insurance salesmen, the real-estate agents, the steamship agents — and the proprietors of junk shops, rag and metal yards, and tourist agencies.

With few important exceptions, most of these people lived a life of grinding poverty, seldom being able to save a dollar; it mattered not how thrifty they were. Naturally, for one of them to donate a dollar for some public purpose meant a great sacrifice. The first organized attempts to help the needy and the unemployed were made by large families and by landsmanschaften groups. They would pool their resources to help a needy relative or a landsman out of work, sometimes even paying the medical fee of a doctor called to look at a sick neighbour not a member of the family group or landsmanschaft.

As economic conditions grew worse the larger families and some of the landsmanschaften groups (people coming from the same town) began to intensify their welfare activities. Voluntary committees were formed for the purpose of visiting the sick and supplying them with medicines. Financial relief, too, was occasionally furnished. Single men out of a job were frequently provided with free board and lodging on the understanding — discreetly arrived at — that the money would be repaid later on. For married people and especially unemployed people with large families there were free gifts of food and groceries. Occasionally a rent bill, long in arrears, was taken care of. In the majority of cases this help — offered in such a way that it didn't hurt or humiliate the recipient — was repaid when work was obtained. Aid was also sometimes given to immigrants wanting to bring their families over from the old country. Private families or landsmanschaften would buy tickets from steamship agencies for those lacking cash and arrange for the money to be paid back in installments of $2 per week.

But things were not rosy all the time. There were occasions when the landsmanschaften had cause to regret their philanthropic impulses. This was particularly true in cases when wives brought to Canada by the landsmanschaften arrived here to discover that they had been deserted by their husbands. There were a good many husbands who would move away to other localities, pass themselves off as single and, not infrequently, marry again. But not all such cases ended tragically. Quite often the landsmanschaften managed to track down the missing husband and bring about a reconciliation. How serious the problem of these desertions was for the Jewish communities in the United States and Canada can be gauged from the amount of space devoted to it by the Yiddish press in those days. Not a single Yiddish paper was published in the United States at the time but that it carried a full page of names of these missing husbands, listing their ages, places of origin and occupations, and very often showing their photographs. More than one such husband later turned up in Toronto.

Role of the Steamship Agents

The first Jewish steamship agents in Toronto were Mr. Louis Rotenberg & Sons, Mr. J. Garfinkel, and Mr. Louis Gurofsky. Not long after these were established, several more agencies were opened, those of Mr. J. J. Kennen, Mr. H. M. Sivitz and Mr. Solomon Heifetz. While booking passages on ocean liners formed the major part of the business of these agencies, a considerable revenue was derived by them from the sale of money orders and other kinds of remittances. From the very first these businesses were quite prosperous. Every second Jew in Toronto had a relative or two in the old country who looked to him for financial assistance. Indeed, many families in the old country were almost wholly dependent on the support they received from this side of the water. On a couple of American dollars a family in Poland or Russia could live for almost a month. The immigrant in Toronto who wanted to send some money home to his parents for Passover or the New Year would naturally go to the Jewish steamship agent to transact his business. With the Jewish agent he could discuss his problems in his own tongue and on his advice he could implicitly rely; so at any rate he felt, and this was quite profitable to the agents. Moreover, the agents received a handsome commission from the steamship lines on each ticket they sold — and most tickets were paid for in Canada. People in Europe seldom had the money to pay for their passage.

Rotenberg & Sons, 1913
The steamship lines paid a handsome commission to their agents on each ticket sold. Rotenberg's (above, right) was located on Queen Street near York in 1913. Below, a 1922 ad in which the company offers assistance in bringing over passengers from Russia.

SOVIET RUSSIA

We can now bring your relatives from Soviet Russia, as well as from Poland and Roumania, and remit to them American or Canadian dollars.

Through our own offices in Warsaw, Lodz, Krakau, Lemberg, Libau, Riga, Kovno, Wilna, Bucharest, etc., we are in the best position to get in direct touch with your passengers and bring them forward promptly by our direct service from Libau and Danzig to Halifax and New York.

Baltic-America Line

Rotenbergs Limited
Canadian General Passenger Agents
TELEPHONES: Adelaide 693, 694, 695
79 QUEEN ST. WEST

That a number of racketeers should appear on the scene and proceed to victimize the more gullible immigrants was almost inevitable. Promising to use special political influence with immigration authorities to get sailing priority for relatives who wished to come to Canada, these unscrupulous individuals would slowly work their way into the confidence of their victim. Then after the money had been handed over, the ingenuous immigrant would wake up one morning to find that agent and money had both disappeared. Such cases were especially common at the beginning and end of the First World War when many Toronto Jews with families in Poland and Russia tried everything — borrowing money from loan societies and even mortgaging their homes — to rescue their dear ones from the war-torn and devastated villages of the old world. There were many such heartbreaking cases in Toronto. Fortunately the agents we mentioned above became more and more widely known in the city — their honesty was unimpeachable — and more and more immigrants turned to them for their needs.

The State of Jewish Education

In 1904 and 1905 signs that a more organized community life was in the offing became more numerous. A new generation of Canadian-educated youngsters was beginning to graduate from the city's public schools. Education was compulsory for children up to the age of fourteen. Children of every nationality and faith were thrown together in the same classroom and school yard. At the most impressionable period of his life the Jewish child was exposed to new influences and new friends — none of them Jewish. Often he came home from school repeating the Christian prayers and hymns he had heard that morning. English words and phrases began to be heard in the Jewish home as often as Yiddish ones. To make themselves understood, parents were more and more forced to try to speak English to their children, quite often with ludicrous results. Their early English speech was a curious hybrid, a bizarre mixture of slang expressions and anglicized Yiddish.

Fearing that their children would entirely forget what little Yiddish they might have known if this process of Canadianization continued for any length of time, some parents began to hire *melamdim* for their children — the European species of private Hebrew teacher. The boys were taught to read *Ivrit* (Hebrew) and to recite the Hebrew prayers, the girls to read

Ward Classroom & Elizabeth Street Playground

Above, Ward-area classroom, ca 1913. Below, Elizabeth Street School playground, 1912, was one of very few places where children could play in the crowded neighbourhood.

and write Yiddish. But few parents could afford to pay the fee, which was sometimes as high as $1 or $1.50 a week. Furthermore, they soon discovered to their deep disquiet that the children had little appetite for studying Hebrew after spending a day at school. And the *melamdim* themselves were no great shakes; those that were available were not always the best nor the most enlightened in their profession.

Moreover, having become accustomed to modern teaching techniques prevailing in the city's public schools and enjoying to the utmost the gay freedom of his new environment, the young Jewish student had little patience with the old-fashioned *melamed* and his archaic ways of teaching. He regarded the bearded stooped figure who came to his home after school hours with a *siddur* and a pointer in his hand as an apparition from a strange and unreal world. The *melamed* usually intoned the lesson in a monotonous sing-song and in a Yiddish that the pupil could sometimes scarcely understand. And the pupil spoke to his teacher in a mixture of English and Yiddish so outlandish that the latter was left completely bewildered. Only a strong sense of duty sometimes kept the parents from calling off what was obviously an unpleasant chore to teacher and pupil alike.

To try to remedy this state of affairs, some of the more intelligent parents sometimes got together to discuss the problem of child education. But little of value came out of these privately held discussions. The community was not yet fully awake to the need of a Jewish school system — that is, one supplementary to the public school system. Moreover, there was the sharpest disagreement among the various groups as to the kind of schools the Jewish community should build. It must be said at this point that the American Yiddish press and the various political groups dominant in local life at the time all bear a large share of the blame for this condition. Each group had a different solution up its sleeve, a solution that harmonized with its own unique social outlook.

The Orthodox, for example, were adamant in their refusal to countenance the creation of a secular Yiddish school. They wanted private *chedarim* modeled on those in the old country. Even the idea of a Talmud Torah was at first distasteful to them. After all, in the old country the Talmud Torah was primarily a charitable institution where the poor and the orphaned were taught free of charge. And the Orthodox were unwilling to see this kind of organization transplanted here to this new country where there should be no need for charity.

The socialists, too, were strongly opposed to the Yiddish secular schools, not to mention the Talmud Torahs. They denounced the former as chauvinistic and the latter as clerical. The socialists, as you know, believed that utopia was just around the corner and that differences between races and nations would swiftly and without too much ado disappear from the face of the earth. All would be brothers, worshipping the same god — socialism. Then why bother perpetuating ancient superstitions and dying nationalisms? The only ones who supported the founding of Yiddish schools were the Socialist Territorialists and the Labour Zionists. And their number was small, their influence almost nil. ✈

Poster, Labor League 10th Anniversary Concert
The celebration was at Massey Hall in November 1936

Pioneers of Congregation Beth Hamidrash Hagadol Chevra Tehillim
Photo ca early 1900s shows (from left): Louis Clavir, Meyer Rubinstein, Pesach Lavine, Alter Blumenfeld, Mendel Gebertig, Reb Zudeck Black, Moishe Clayman, Feivish Hoffstein, Moishe Ber Clavir. The congregation had a large synagogue on McCaul Street.

※ 4 ※

Synagogues, Congregations & Rabbis

WHEREVER JEWS SETTLED in any numbers the pattern of their organizational beginnings was always pretty much the same. The first act of the new arrivals was to transplant the Orthodox shul into the new land and acquire a cemetery of their own. In Upper Canada too the first immigrants, shortly after their arrival, proceeded to establish their own organized community life, founding a congregation and acquiring ground for a cemetery. In this chapter we intend to speak of the origins and growth of many synagogues of the Toronto Jewish community and to describe some of the struggles and ambitions of the early founders. As the largest group in the community has always been the religious, we shall devote ourselves

Nordheimer Pianos, King Street, 1846

The first location of the music house of A. & S. Nordheimer was on the north side of King Street between Yonge and Toronto Streets.

chiefly to the Orthodox institutions, only briefly sketching in the history of the Reform congregations.

Many of the Jewish residents of Toronto in the first half of the nineteenth century were of German origin and though we might expect them to have been followers of the Reform movement then spreading across Germany, the majority of them were, as a matter of fact, intensely Orthodox. In the book *One Hundred Years in Toronto*, published by the Toronto City Council to mark the city's centenary in 1934, it is reported that in the year 1851 there were 103 Jews in Upper Canada (Ontario), of whom 57 lived in Toronto.

Abraham Rhinewine, reviewing the early history of the Jews in Canada, writes: "We learn from the diaries of the Davids that Wellington Hart along with certain other Jews already lived in Upper Canada at the beginning of the nineteenth century." Among the first pioneers to reside in Toronto and other Ontario localities were the Benjamin brothers in Toronto, the brothers Abraham and Herman Levy in Hamilton, and the families Freedman, Cohen and Jacobs in Lancaster. The German Jewish family of Nordheimer was also one of the first Jewish families in Toronto, but through intermarriage its descendants have disappeared out of the Jewish community.

Abraham Nordheimer, born in Bavaria, came to Canada from New York where he had received some recognition as a musician. While living in New York where he had arrived in 1939 he became the friend of General Torens, the commander of a regiment stationed in Kingston, Upper Canada. General Torens persuaded Nordheimer to go to Canada, there to teach music to the children of the Governor General Sir Charles Bagot. Shortly afterwards, in the 1840s, Abraham Nordheimer's younger brother, Samuel, followed him to Toronto, and together the two brothers founded the music house of A. & S. Nordheimer. In 1869, Abraham Nordheimer died while on a visit to his native Bavaria.

The First Reform Congregation

Although the Hughson Street Temple (Anshe Shalom) in Hamilton, Ontario, which Edmond Scheuer and Mark Cohen helped to establish in 1882, was the first Reform synagogue to be built in Canada, the first Reform congregation in Toronto was formed as early as September 1856. This was the ancestor of the present Holy Blossom. In that year a small group of people banded together and founded a place of worship for the High Holy Days. The first elected officers of the Congregation, which was then called Sons of Israel, were: Mr. Joseph Lyons, chairman; Mr. A. Aarons, secretary; Mr. S. Behrends, treasurer; Messrs. L. Levine and M. Levy, trustees. For more than twenty years a quorum of members held services in a room located above Coomb's Drug Store at the corner of Yonge and Richmond Streets, for which the handsome rental of $4 per week was paid. For the high holiday services, a sefer Torah and, presumably, a shofar were borrowed from the Montreal Reform congregation, whose spiritual leader then was Rabbi Abraham de Sola. The first *shamus* of the shul was a certain Mr. Joseph who received the grand salary of $50 a year plus a 5% commission on all the monies collected. Mr. Goldberg, a former resident of Buffalo, combined the functions of reader, *shoichet* and *mohel* at a yearly stipend of $75.

Small membership, irregular attendance and limited funds hampered the growth of the congregation for some twenty years, from 1856 to 1879, and it was sometimes necessary to engage, at a small salary, a person to act simultaneously as cantor, reader, teacher, *mohel*, *shoichet* and *shamus*. However, from this small quorum of regular worshippers there evolved

Richmond Street Synagogue (Holy Blossom), 1875 to 1897

Worshippers faced south in the first purpose-built synagogue in Toronto, located on the south side of Richmond at Victoria. Interior (below) shows women's balconies, rosette windows, and Hebrew phrase over Holy Ark: "Know Before Whom You Stand."

the first shul in Toronto, known as the Toronto Hebrew Congregation or Holy Blossom. This second name was used officially as early as 1862, and is still retained today by its successor, the Holy Blossom Congregation.

In an interesting article under the title "History of the Holy Blossom Congregation" in the souvenir book issued to commemorate the opening of the new Holy Blossom Temple (1938) on Bathurst Street, Mr. Mark Cohen, a former president of the congregation, writes that "the earliest reference to Jewish settlement in York (the name of which was changed to Toronto in 1834) dates back to 1817." He lists the names of a number of early Jewish residents of the city, adding that though some of them came from Germany, most were of English origin, their ancestors having some centuries earlier come to England from Spain and Holland.

He cites an entry in the records of the registry office under the date of September 1, 1849, "wherein the Hon. John Beverly Robinson conveyed to Judah G. Joseph and Abraham Nordheimer, merchants, trustees of the Hebrew Congregation of Toronto, lands on the east side of Centre Road (now Pape Avenue) for use as a burial ground for the sum of £20 currency." According to Mr. Rhinewine, the ground for the cemetery, the first property owned by the Jewish community in Toronto, was acquired many years before the first synagogue was built here. The names of some of the early Jews in Toronto are found inscribed on the tombstones marking the graves of Simon Alfred Joseph (died Sept. 17, 1850); Lewis, son of Joseph Lyons (d. Feb. 1, 1851); J. G. Joseph (d. May 12, 1852); and Charlotte, daughter of Abraham and Fannie Nordheimer (d. Sept. 27, 1855, at the age of nine).

➣ *The Richmond Street Synagogue*

About 1875, through the assistance of Mr. Lewis Samuels, a parcel of land on Richmond Street one block east of Yonge Street was purchased for $6,000 and the Richmond Street Synagogue, as it was then called, was erected on this site, later the site of the Victoria Theatre. Messrs. Lewis Samuel, Alexander Miller, Marcus Green and Max Kassel were among the trustees of the synagogue. With the erection of the new building, with a larger membership and increased revenues, the congregation began to thrive. In 1879, Rabbi Joseph Gluck, a trained cantor, was engaged as pastor and he served in that capacity until 1882. Under his leadership a ladies' choir was formed and instrumental music introduced. Before that time the services had been conducted in the ultra-Orthodox manner: there was not even mixed seating, a separate section being partitioned off for the use of ladies. Only gradually were reforms, very slight at first, introduced into the Orthodox ritual and liturgy.

In his *Toronto from Trading Post to Great City*, E. C. Guillet describes the first synagogue in these words: "The first Jewish synagogue in Toronto was on the south side of Richmond Street, a short distance east of Victoria. The interior was not greatly different from that of Christian churches, consisting of main floor and galleries. About 125 persons made up the congregation of this synagogue in 1886, and it was known by the name of Holy Blossom."

In 1883, Cantor Herman Phillips succeeded Rabbi Gluck and occupied the position of rabbi and cantor until 1890. The first ordained English-speaking rabbi to minister to the congregation was Dr. Barnet A. Elzas, a graduate of Jews' College, London, who came to the Holy Blossom pulpit in 1890. His attempts to introduce further reforms met with strong opposition; some members resigned to join the Goel Tzedec Congregation that had been founded in the meantime, and others who remained continued to obstruct his program of reform. Discouraged by the prolonged friction, Rabbi Elzas resigned in 1893 and was succeeded by Abraham Lazarus, B.A., who was also a graduate of Jews' College, London. Rabbi Lazarus was a fiery orator and a good teacher and was responsible for introducing the Friday evening services at which men and women could sit together.

The Bond Street Synagogue

A campaign for money to build a new synagogue was started in 1893 and in 1895 — when the membership was a mere 119 — a site on Bond Street was purchased for $7,200. The first services in the completed new synagogue were held on Rosh Hashana, September 15, 1897. In 1899, when the membership objected to the use of the organ at services and the reading of the prayers in English, Rabbi Lazarus resigned after serving as spiritual head of the congregation for five years. He was succeeded by Rabbi David N. Wittenberg of New York, who occupied the pulpit until August, 1900. Rabbi Isaac Landman, also of Manhattan, was the next incumbent and remained until 1901.

Holy Blossom on Bond Street, 1897 to 1937

The congregation numbered only 119 members in 1895 when it purchased the site on which it would build this grand and confident structure, its home for 40 years.

In 1901 Rabbi Solomon Jacobs was accepted as the new spiritual leader. Born in Sheffield, England, Rabbi Jacobs had previously been appointed minister of the United Congregations of Kingston, Jamaica, upon the recommendation of the Chief Rabbi of England. The venerable rabbi was revered and loved by the membership and esteemed by the community at large. During the First World War he acted as chaplain in various military camps and on all occasions he revealed a strong sense of British patriotism. He served the Bond Street Congregation for nineteen years until his death in 1920.

With the arrival of large numbers of East European immigrants with their deeper religious consciousness, and with new Orthodox synagogues springing up everywhere, the gulf between the Reform and the Orthodox sections of the community widened. The services in the Bond Street Synagogue became in the meantime much more reformed. In 1903 the playing of the organ on the High Holy days was introduced and music began to take an increasingly important part in the services. A school for the religious education of the English-speaking children was established, to be guided for more than thirty years by the much loved Mr. Edmund Scheuer.

In the meantime the cultural ties with American Jewry (as distinguished from English Jewry) were growing stronger. Since the death of Rabbi Jacobs in 1920 the incumbents of the Holy Blossom pulpit have all been graduates of the Hebrew Union College of Cincinnati. The first of these was Rabbi Barnet A. Brickner, who was appointed in 1920. In the five years that he was pastor the Reform elements were intensified and the ancient ritual radically changed. Rabbi Brickner introduced the Union Prayer Book, abolished separate seating for men and women, and severed the last links with the Orthodox and Conservative congregations. In 1923 he was succeeded by Rabbi Ferdinand Isserman who occupied the pulpit until 1929. Rabbi Isserman used his high office to appeal for aid for the underprivileged, and was the first to introduce Sunday morning services into the Temple.

In 1929 Rabbi Maurice N. Eisendrath took over and served with distinction for many years. A brilliant orator, he attracted wide attention with his comments and many Christians came to attend his services at the Holy Blossom.

Seeking to emphasize the religious ideals common to both Jew and Gentile, he introduced the practice of exchanging pulpits with eminent Christian clergymen. In addition, he conducted *Forum of the Air*, a weekly Sunday afternoon sermon broadcast over a number of radio stations. At first Rabbi Eisendrath was a sharp critic of Jewish nationalism but he was converted to Zionism after a visit to Palestine. He became a warm supporter of the Histadrut and aided in its campaign for funds. When he retired from the pulpit of the Holy Blossom Synagogue he left behind a host of friends and admirers both in the Jewish community and in the city at large. At present he is the president of the Union of American Hebrew Congregations.

The neighbourhood in which the Bond Street Synagogue had been located since 1897 had in the course of time deteriorated, with the members moving away to newer districts and coming long distances to attend services. The building itself had become inadequate for the needs of the larger membership. In March 1937, the site for the new Temple on Bathurst Street was purchased for $26,500 and the old Bond Street building was sold to the Hellenic Orthodox Church. The congregation held its last service in the old synagogue on September 27, 1937.

The Holy Blossom Temple

The new Holy Blossom Temple with Maurice N. Eisendrath as Rabbi opened its doors at a dedication ceremony held on May 20, 1938. The Temple occupied an entire block on Bathurst Street, between Ava Road and Dewbourne Avenue, and is in the centre of one of the city's new fashionable residential districts. Constructed in monolithic concrete and architecturally modeled on Romanesque design, the new edifice is a beautiful and imposing modern landmark in the city.

Rabbi Abraham L. Fineberg, who was born and brought up in an Orthodox home, came to the Holy Blossom Temple in November, 1943 and has since been the spiritual head of the congregation. A liberal thinker and a brilliant orator, Rabbi Fineberg has, by his devotion to the cause of Judaism and by his energetic participation in communal activities, won a lasting place for himself in the hearts and minds of the members of the Jewish community.

A political progressive and a devoted Zionist at the same time, Rabbi Fineberg has gained a wide audience for himself through his challenging sermons on topical subjects. His opinions on questions as diverse as religious education in the public school and whether Jerusalem should be internationalized are heard

Construction photograph, 1937

Sanctuary of Holy Blossom Temple
Built by architects Chapman & Oxley, already celebrated for such landmark buildings as the Princes' Gates, Royal Ontario Museum and Eaton's College Street.

with respect and have had, it is widely believed, a constructive influence on public sentiment.

The adherents of the early Reform movement regarded themselves as Canadian citizens of the Mosaic faith and spurned all claims to separate Jewish nationhood; they held out very little or no appeal to the masses. The Orthodox shunned contact with the Holy Blossom, considering the reformed liturgy and ritual a repudiation of traditional Judaism; and many others opposed the militant anti-Zionism of the reformers, seeing in the assimilationist ideology of the Reform Jew a threat to Jewish national survival. Recently, however, the Holy Blossom Temple under the more dynamic leadership of Rabbi Fineberg has begun to show a greater appreciation of traditional values: it has reintroduced Sabbath services and brought back Hebrew to the ritual.

The Rise of Landsmanschaft Organizations

There was a new stream of immigration into Canada in the 1880s and many of the newcomers settled in Toronto. According to E. C. Guillet in his book *Toronto from Trading Post to Great City*, the Jewish population of Toronto during those years grew slowly but steadily. "Jews numbered 1,425 in 1891 and 3,078 in 1901," he says. "At that time the only Jewish synagogues [*aside from Holy Blossom*] were three small buildings which served chiefly three small groups of Austrian, Polish or Russian Jews."

From that time on the new immigrants were almost always from Russia, Poland, Lithuania and Galicia, and were largely Orthodox. They came to Canada bringing the customs and traditions of the old country. Before long the neighbourhood bounded by Yonge Street on the east and University Avenue on the west was populated chiefly by Jews; and Elm, Elizabeth, Edward, Chestnut, Centre, Teraulay and Simcoe streets (today's downtown area) were bustling with immigrant life. Small stores, little tailoring establishments, dry-goods shops and rag and metal yards sprang up all over the neighbourhood, providing work for many of the immigrants.

Gradually attempts were made to organize the religious life of the small but growing community. Because many of the newcomers desired to retain as much as possible of the old way of life, they tended to form separate congregations pertaining to many cities from the old country; many of these early Orthodox congregations were of the landsmanschaft variety, consisting of former residents of the same home town. When we later enumerate the various small congregations we shall see that their names generally echo the places of origin of their members.

The younger immigrants, most of them married and impecunious, left their countries and their families and came here hoping to accumulate enough money to be able either to return home slightly more affluent or to remain and send for their wives and children. It was natural for them to seek out and associate with their landsleit or countrymen not only because they had the same memories but also so that they might help one another in the new world. When there were enough landsleit to form a *minyan* (a quorum of ten adults, the minimum requirement for the performance of religious services) they would rent a room and use it as a synagogue and occasionally as a place for social gatherings. At first these *minyanim* were of three distinct linguistic classes and their members bore nicknames in accordance with the country of their origin. The "Kossacks" consisted of Russian and Lithuanian Jews; the "Greitzer" consisted of Galician Jews (Galicia being the part of Poland annexed to Austria); and the "Dropkes" consisted of Jews who came from Poland.

⇒ *Shomrei Shabbos & Rabbi Joseph Weinreb*

The first of the East European immigrants to organize a congregation and to make plans for bringing an Orthodox rabbi over from Europe were the Galician Jews, many of them scholarly and pious men anxious to raise their children in the Orthodox tradition. Some of them were *maskilim* (adherents of the *Haskalah*, a movement for Jewish enlightenment popular in the nineteenth century) and disciples of Nachman Krochmal, Isaac Ertes, Joseph Perl and S. I. Rappaport, intellectual leaders who sought to harmonize the teachings of Judaism with the liberalism of modern thought. Others were followers of Hassidism, a democratic folk movement of immense spiritual vitality that was founded by Rabbi Israel Baal Shem Tov and spread by his devoted disciples.

Because of their small numbers the early Galician Jewish immigrants buried their ideological differences and formed a congregation called Shomrei Shabbos, the Guardians of the Law. According to Mr. Pesach Edell, one of the first Jewish printers in Toronto and a member of the congregation from its inception, the Shomrei Shabbos was founded in

1898 with a membership of eleven, mostly door-to-door salesmen and rag peddlers. The first president of the congregation was Mr. Leibish Gelber, its first spiritual head Rabbi Isaac Halpern, a *shoichet*. Its services were conducted in a room located at 61 Chestnut Street, then in larger quarters at 125 Queen Street West.

With larger membership and increased revenues the congregation next bought two houses located at 109–111 Chestnut Street, remodeling them and establishing the Shomrei Shabbos Synagogue, the first Orthodox synagogue in Toronto. The first elected officers of the new congregation were Messrs. Moses Brody and Moses Gelber, president and secretary respectively. With the acquisition of the new building, the members decided to engage an Orthodox rabbi and after considering a number of candidates, selected Rabbi Joseph Weinreb, a native of Busk, Galicia, inviting him in 1899 to come to Toronto to be the spiritual leader of the congregation.

Rabbi Weinreb, who was at this time the religious head of the Jewish community in Jassy, Roumania, had received his *s'micha* or rabbinical ordination from the Brejaner Rabbi, a famed author of many authoritative books on Jewish law. Although his position in the Jassy community had brought him many honours, Rabbi Weinreb was moved by the appeals of his landsleit in Toronto, who pleaded with him to accept the leadership of their congregation. On his arrival in Toronto in 1900 he became rabbi of the Shomrei Shabbos and remained head of the congregation until his death in 1943.

❧ *Some Early Documents of Historical Interest*

The financial standing of the Toronto Jewish community at the beginning of the century and the economic status of the rabbi can be gauged from reading several interesting early documents which have fortunately been preserved.

Formerly when a rabbi was appointed, it was customary to draw up a document called the *Ketab Rabbanuth* or the "Writ of Rabbinate." This writ eulogizing the rabbi and the agreement that accompanied it were written in a mixture of Hebrew and Aramaic and specified in detail the duties and obligations of the rabbi as well as his rights and privileges. The contract between Rabbi Weinreb and members of his congregation was the first contract of its kind signed in Toronto. Translated, it reads as follows:

We the undersigned members of the Congregation Shomrei Shabbos, Men of Austria, whose signatures are affixed below, hereby agreed to accept as our rabbi and spiritual head the learned and scholarly Rabbi Weinreb. We also agree to pay the said rabbi the sum of $300 a year, such sum to be paid out of the treasury of this Congregation in twelve equal payments of $25 a month. This contract is declared to be valid and binding according to the laws of the country and shall continue in force for a period of three years commencing from the date of Rabbi Weinreb's assumption of office. We the undersigned, the duly authorized representatives of the congregation, do hereby acknowledge the said obligation on behalf of the Shomrei Shabbos Congregation.

Of the thirty-two members who affixed their signatures to the contract only four are still living [1950]. Among the signers were Messrs. Moses Brody, Moses Gelber, Leibish Gelber, Isaac Shub and Benjamin Kurtz.

The Gelbers mentioned here were members of a family prominent in Jewish affairs in Galicia, a family that produced many distinguished scholars and writers. The Toronto branch of this family has become equally distinguished in many fields, with all of them playing prominent roles in Toronto Jewish life. It can be said, with a good deal of justification, that these thirty-two Galician Jews laid the foundations of organized Jewish Orthodox life in Toronto. Many of their descendants, who today are prominent in the city's economic life, follow in the path of their parents and take an active part in the affairs of the Jewish community.

The synagogue on Chestnut Street was sold many years ago, the building eventually becoming the location of a rag and metal yard. A few years ago workers found in the cellar of this old building a sealed jar containing a document of historical interest. This document, dating back to 1899, is written in Hebrew and bears the following message:

Benjamin Kurtz, a shoichet, with Rabbi Weinreb (seated)

Orthodox Rabbis in March, Toronto, ca 1915
Rabbi Joseph Weinreb, centre, appears to be listening to man with outstretched hand, possibly Rabbi Yudel Rosenberg. Behind them is Rabbi Jacob Gordon in top hat.

This message is written for posterity. We, the undersigned, members of a committee elected to represent the Shomrei Shabbos Congregation, Men of Austria whose signatures are affixed below, bear witness that we have been empowered by the membership to name our synagogue the "Shomrei Shabbos, Men of Austria" and we wish it to be known that it is forbidden for any person or persons to alter the said name or in any way to modify the liturgy of the congregation. We also state that the religious ways of this congregation must adhere closely to those of our ancestors in Poland and be forever strictly Orthodox. The cornerstone of this building was laid by Leibish Gelber, the learned and eminent son of Nathan Gelber of Bresian, Galicia.

The document was signed by Messrs. Joseph B. Tugenhaft, Samuel L. Levinter, S. D. Garfinkle, I. Isaac, Zelig Brodey and Rabbi Isaac Halpern. Preceding the last signature, there appears the name "Rev. I. Halpern, 106 Albert Street, Toronto" stamped in English. According to information in the Jubilee Book issued by the Talmud Torah Eitz Chaim, Rabbi I. Halpern, who was a shoichet, acted as religious leader of the Shomrei Shabbos Congregation until the arrival of Rabbi Weinreb. A postscript, written by Mr. Brody, president of the congregation, follows:

The undersigned bear witness that this document was composed at the request of the membership of the Shomrei Shabbos Congregation and was approved by them. Signed by me on March 8, 1899, and witnessed by Moses Brody, president of the congregation.

❧ Machzikei Hadat

A few years after Shomrei Shabbos was established, a serious controversy split the congregation into two rival camps. The immediate cause of this was the application for membership made by persons who were known to work on the Sabbath day. The more pious elements of the congregation stubbornly opposed their admission, regarding those who violated the Sabbath as unfit for membership. The more progressive, on the other hand, welcomed the newcomers, arguing that harsh necessity forced many to work on the Sabbath who were otherwise deeply religious. The dispute grew sharper and feeling in the congregation ran high until, finally, a group consisting of the most Orthodox members broke away from the congregation. At a stormy meeting held on May 6, 1906, a resolution calling for the establishment of a new congregation was introduced by Mr. Moses Gelber and approved by the majority. That very year this group founded a separate congregation which they called the Machzikei Hadat, the Fortifiers of the Faith, and almost immediately they built the splendid synagogue that stood until 1944 at 105 Teraulay street. (Today this street is part of Bay Street, one of the city's main arteries.) Mr. S. Frohlich was the first president of the new synagogue and was succeeded by Mr. Moses Gelber, who remained president for many years.

Although he sided with the Machzikei Hadat, departing with them to their new location, Rabbi Weinreb continued his association with the older Shomrei Shabbos. Though not particularly brilliant as an orator, Rabbi Weinreb was a rabbi in the best European tradition. A Talmudic scholar, he was not a recluse but accessible to the masses; a man of deep learning, he was at the same time profoundly interested in the practical welfare of his congregation. He was unbendingly Orthodox and shunned the *Maskalah* with its modern teachings, believing that a Jew should observe all the traditional laws and customs. A tolerant man, he refused to become involved in communal controversies, striving always to be fair and just. Although he was only too qualified to make religious decisions

 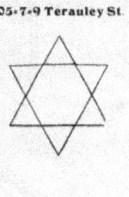

Machzikei Hadat letterhead

independently, Rabbi Weinreb never hesitated to consult the opinions of other rabbis, and a number of his questions and answers on religious matters are contained in the book written by his distinguished colleague, Rabbi Yehuda Leib Graubart.

Until the arrival of Rabbi Graubart about 1920, Rabbi Weinreb was considered the chief Orthodox rabbi of Toronto and his authority in religious matters went unquestioned in the community. When the Talmud Torah Eitz Chaim, consisting chiefly of Polish Jews, celebrated its second anniversary on August 11, 1918, Rabbi Weinreb shared top honours with Rabbi Yudel Rosenberg, the spiritual head of the Polish congregations. Always interested in Jewish education and community welfare, he helped to organize the first schools and the first benevolent societies. He was a modest and retiring man deeply respected and loved by the community. He died in 1943 at the age of seventy-seven, after forty-three years as a rabbi in Toronto.

Quite a number of congregations in Toronto were founded by Galician Jews, including many members of the original Shomrei Shabbos Synagogue. This group comprised the Shomrei Shabbos at Brunswick and Sussex, the Men of the Husatianer Klaus, the Agudath Achim, the Men of Narayever, and the Strettiner Beth Hamidrash.

The present membership of Shomrei Shabbos is 170. Although the majority is still of Galician origin the congregation now includes quite a number of Polish and Lithuanian worshippers. These have joined for various reasons, some because they live in the neighbourhood and the synagogues of their own landsleit are too far to walk to on the Sabbath days; others because having married the daughters of Galician Jews, they prefer to attend the same synagogue as their in-laws.

Goel Tzedec — University Avenue Synagogue — 1924
With a capacity for 1,200, the landmark synagogue had an exquisite interior and was perhaps the city's finest looking Jewish house of worship. Erected 1906, demolished 1955.

⌑ Goel Tzedec Congregation

As time passed, the divisions among the Galician, Polish, Russian and Lithuanian Jews began to be less and less important. The immigrants' clannishness diminished as they became more integrated into their new environment and relaxed their habit of maintaining separate congregations for people of different places of origin. In addition, the movement of the Jewish population to newer sections of the city hastened the trend towards heterogeneous congregations, since many found it difficult if not impossible to walk on Saturdays to the older synagogues.

Thus, for example, many immigrants, Polish as well as Russian, had joined the Goel Tzedec Congregation, which was founded in 1883. Its first services were conducted in rented quarters on Richmond Street. To accommodate the additional worshippers on the High Holy days, it was necessary for the congregation to rent the Temperance Hall for a period of three days. In 1884, the members of the Goel Tzedec bought a church at the corner of Elm Street and University Avenue, remodeling it into the synagogue that stood on this corner for more than twenty-three years.

The present imposing synagogue of the Goel Tzedec congregation, a historic landmark in the city located at 97 University Avenue, was built in 1906. The cornerstone of the new building was laid on April 29 of that year and the new synagogue formally dedicated on February 3, 1907. The first rabbi of the Goel Tzedec was Rabbi Jacob Gordon and upon his retirement he was succeeded by Rabbis Julius J. Price, J. S. Siegel and Jesse Schwartz. In 1916, a sisterhood was established under the capable leadership of Mrs. Ida Siegel.

In 1927, Rabbi Samuel Sachs came to the congregation's pulpit and largely because of his great popularity in the community the membership of the synagogue grew by leaps and bounds. For reasons of health, Rabbi Sachs had to retire from the congregation after seventeen years as its spiritual head. He left for California, where he now lives. His devotion to the welfare of the congregation and his labours on behalf of the Jewish community as a whole won him a multitude of friends and admirers. Upon his retirement he was succeeded by Rabbi Perlzweig, an Englishman, and later by Rabbi Norman Shapiro, who came here from Tulsa, Oklahoma. In Toronto, the Goel Tzedec was regarded as a Conservative congregation. The Conservative movement was an attempt to modernize traditional

Rare Photograph of Former Elm Street Synagogue, ca 1908
The building was Goel Tzedec's home from 1884 to 1907. It was sold and converted into the city's first Yiddish theatre, but closed permanently after the balcony collapsed in 1908.

Judaism without breaking with its essential beliefs and practices; it was strongly opposed to the extreme ideology of the Reform movement.

The present incumbent in the Goel Tzedec is Rabbi Norman Shapiro. Cantor Akiva Bernstein is in charge of the choir, Mr. Eric Feldheim is the educational director, Mr. Bert Godfrey is the president of the congregation, and Judge Samuel Factor chairman of the board of directors. Other officers are Mr. Charles Foster, vice-president; Mr. Ellis I. Shapiro, parnos; Dr. M. L. Simon, gabbai; Mr. Louis M. Posluns, treasurer; and Mr. H. R. Fox, secretary. The congregation is now seeking to build a new synagogue in the northern part of the city and plans have been drawn up to make it architecturally the most impressive Conservative synagogue in Toronto.

⇒ Beth Hamidrash HaGadol Chevra Tehillim

Parallel with the development of the Shomrei Shabbos congregation of the Galician Jews was the development of the Congregation Beth Hamidrash HaGadol Chevra Tehillim of the Russian and Lithuanian Jews. This congregation is popularly known as the McCaul Street Synagogue. In 1938 the McCaul Street congregation celebrated its fiftieth anniversary, publishing for the occasion a very interesting souvenir pamphlet edited by Mr. S. Traub. Mr. Traub says in his introduction that unfortunately no systematic records of the synagogue's history have been kept so that it was necessary for him to piece out the story with reminiscences by individual members. He also mentions the fact that whereas the other early Toronto Orthodox synagogues were of a landsmanschaft character, the McCaul Street congregation was of a more heterogeneous composition from the very first.

The congregation initially known as Chevra Tehillim was founded in 1887. Among the first members, none of whom are alive today, were Mr. Chaim Wilder, Mr. Chaim N. Barasch, Mr. Samuel L. Levinter and Mr. Abraham Brody — men close in spirit to each other though coming from different geographical localities. The services were held at first in an upper storey above Mr. Brody's food store at the corner of York and Richmond Streets. In 1896 the congregation was transferred to new quarters on Richmond Street. In 1898, eleven years after the Chevra Tehillim was founded, it became necessary to remodel these new quarters for the congregation's membership had substantially increased in the interval. The job was expected to cost about $300, a considerable sum at that time. Mr. Samuel L. Levinter provided this sum in exchange for the privilege of having the congregation renamed Chevra Tehillim Beth Samuel in his honour. Although the majority of members approved of the renaming at first, a majority later thought better of it, and Mr. Levinter graciously released the congregation from its commitment. Meanwhile, the congregation decided to raise money by bringing in an eminent American cantor for the High Holidays. This proved a great success and the congregation netted $850 through ticket sales. The cantor, who hailed from Rochester, was Rabbi L. Shochet. He was assisted by the congregation's own cantor, Rabbi Yudel (Julius) Breslin.

Although he did not succeed in having his name appended to the name of the congregation, Mr. Levinter nevertheless footed the bill of $300 for the alterations on the understanding that a portion of *mishnayos* would be studied every year on his *yahrzeit*, the anniversary of his death. This was done, but the congregation solemnly resolved at the same time that the words Chevra Tehillim should never be removed from the congregation's full title. The name of Mr. Samuel Levinter, this early benefactor of the congregation, was engraved on the synagogue's marble memorial tablet.

The membership of the Chevra Tehilim grew from year to year, increasing from forty in 1898 to many hundreds in later years. In 1899 a

The McCaul Street building as a Methodist church in the 1890s

grocery building was purchased at the corner of Simcoe and Pearl streets for $4,500 and transformed into a synagogue. Four years later the building was sold for $6,500 and the congregation recognized another substantial profit.

In 1904, the congregation bought a large church on McCaul street for $30,000 with a down payment of $5,000. This church was converted into one of the Jewish community's most important religious centres. To reflect the large size of its new home, the congregation renamed itself Beth Hamidrash Hagadol Chevra Tehillim. In 1905 a dedication service was held to mark its opening with Rabbi Jacob Gordon, Rabbi Joseph Weinreb, Rabbi Solomon Jacobs and the synagogue's newly appointed cantor, Mr. Schulman, delivering the dedicatory addresses. Many prominent Toronto Jews were among the first members of the McCaul Street Synagogue.

Representatives of the synagogue took a leading part in the creation of

View of McCaul Street Synagogue, ca 1920s
Chevra Tehillim Congregation renamed itself Beth Hamidrash HaGadol Chevra Tehillim when it moved into the former church, McCaul Street at Grange, in 1905.

the Toronto *Kehilla*, the central religious organization for the city, when it was formed in 1922. Numerous of the synagogue's delegates, including Mr. M. D. Clavir (head of the prominent Clavir family), Mr. L. Pollec, Mr. S. Breslin, Mr. S. Reider and Mr. Samuel Levinter, took on important administrative responsibilities in the new body; as did Mr. Elias Pullan of Goel Tzedec. In 1926 the eminent Mr. Bernard Wladowsky was appointed cantor of the synagogue and he has held the post to this day. It has been a tradition of the synagogue to appoint someone to lecture once a week to the members on a Biblical text. The first so appointed was Rabbi Jacob Gordon; the next, Mr. M. D. Clavir, and later Mr. Zalkind Mittel, *shoichet*. The synagogue's more active members during the half century of its existence included Mr. Max Clavir, Mr. Samuel L. Levinter, Mr. Solomon Breslin, the Gebirtigs, Mr. J. M. Pullan and Mr. Max Axler.

Since Rabbi Gordon's death, and particularly since Rabbi Reuben Slonim, a graduate of the Jewish Theological Seminary of New York became its rabbi, the McCaul Street Synagogue has become Conservative rather than Orthodox — in the senses distinguished above. The congregation has more than 500 members now. Its president is Mr. Morris B. Kaufman.

Rabbi Jacob Gordon, z"l

For many years the religious head of both the Goel Tzedec and the Beth Hamidrash HaGadol Chevra Tehillim congregations was Rabbi Jacob Gordon, who was born in Russia in 1877 and who died in Toronto on November 25, 1934. Originally Rabbi Gordon came to Toronto in 1904 in the interests of the Volozhiner Yeshiva where he had been a student. He liked the city and stayed on as head of Goel Tzedec, the Beth Hamidrash Hagadol Chevra Tehillim and numerous other synagogues. Rabbi Gordon was a scholar and author of

Rare early photo of Rabbi Gordon, 1913, reproduced from Yiddish newspaper

outstanding merit, a man of wide secular as well as Talmudic knowledge. Friendly and approachable, he exercised a deep influence on the Toronto of his day and on the rest of the province as well. Rabbi Gordon helped to organize the Simcoe Street Talmud Torah (Eitz Chaim) and later its successor, the Brunswick Avenue Talmud Torah (Associated). He personally taught in the latter school, and he was the man who introduced the study of oral Hebrew — *Ivrit b'Ivrit* — into its classes.

In 1919 Rabbi Gordon was one of those instrumental in organizing the Canadian Jewish Congress. Later he was one of the founders of the Mizrachi, the religious Zionist organization. He was active in many social and welfare activities and after the First World War he helped to bring into Canada many orphaned children. A fervent Zionist and staunchly Orthodox, he naturally opposed the Reform movement and the rabbis who preached sermons on Christianity. He also battled the radical elements in the community, those who openly flouted the teaching of Orthodoxy.

Besides being spiritual leader of the Goel Tzedec and McCaul Street congregations, Rabbi Gordon was rabbi of the Shearith Israel, Tzemach Tzedek (Lubavitch), Yavneh Zionist and the Knesseth Israel congregations; the latter is on Maria Street in the West Toronto Junction.

The Rise of the "Anshei" Congregations

Like many other Jewish communities in the new world, the organized Toronto Jewish community emerged out of the small landsleit organizations that sprang up in the city with each new incoming wave of immigrants. Although European Jews began to go to America in considerable numbers as early as the 1880s, the great mass migration — the greatest in Jewish history — intensified in 1900 and lasted until 1914, then resumed for several years after 1918, with millions of Jews leaving Eastern and Central Europe to seek new homes in North and South America.

This movement of Jewish migration took place historically in three stages. The first stage was the exodus from Russia in the 1880s when an outbreak of savage pogroms shook the Jewish population to its depths. The second stage was in the first years of this century, after the outbreak of the Russo-Japanese war and the attempted assassination of the Czar. Fear of reprisals spread through Russia; many believed that the Czarist authorities would not stop with the suppression of the revolutionary movement but would wreak further vengeance upon the Jewish population, which it had always used as a scapegoat when it wished to divert the discontent of the masses from itself. The third stage came at the end of the First World War when the economic situation in Poland (and renewed pogroms in Ukraine) forced many Jews to leave those countries and travel overseas.

A good many of those who forsook Europe during these three periods of mass migration came to Canada, with large numbers establishing themselves in Toronto. The newcomers were artisans and small traders who only very slowly adjusted themselves to Canadian conditions. In time they developed the garment industry and came to take a predominant part in building up the retail trades. Shortly after their arrival in Toronto the immigrants began to organize themselves into societies, congregations and landsmanschaften. The purpose of the landsmanschaften and "anshei's" was to keep alive among the immigrants a consciousness of their common origins and a feeling for the ancient traditional way of life.

The familiar Yiddish greeting *"Fun vanet kumt a yid?"* ("Where does a Jew hail from?") is often heard even today, when old immigrants meet and a nostalgic longing for the old country is momentarily kindled by these encounters, which never fail to produce an animated bit of conversation about the old home town. The anshei's, the *chevra's*, and the congregations founded by the immigrants became the nucleii of the early landsmanschaften. During the First World War and the years immediately after, the assistance furnished by these landsmanschaften substantially helped in the rehabilitation of the devastated towns of Poland.

The third stage of emigration consisted of Polish Jews chiefly, with large numbers of those that poured out of the small Polish towns after the First World War coming to Toronto. With their arrival a fresh and vigorous spirit was injected into the life of the local community and there came about a strong revival of religious orthodoxy. Numerous synagogues and *klausen* (small storefront synagogues, also known as *shtiblach*) sprang up all over the Jewish neighbourhood. Whenever a sufficient number of Polish Jews coming from the same small town got together, they founded a congregation and named it after the town they had left behind. Thus there sprang up the Anshei Chmelnik on Huron Street, the Anshei Yivansk on D'Arcy Street, the Anshei Shidlov on D'Arcy Street, the Anshei Apt on Beverley Street, the Anshei Drildge on Markham and Ulster Streets, the Anshei Keltz (headed by Rabbi Tsvi Silverstein) on Dundas Street, the Anshei Ostrovtze on Elizabeth Street, the Anshei Slipye on Chestnut Street, and many others.

The Anshei Slipye was founded in 1908 and the congregation, called the Chevra Knesseth Yisroel Anshei Slipye, had its first shul on Chestnut Street. There were forty-six members at the beginning and Mr. Abraham Luftspring was the first president. The congregation today numbers sixty-two and Mr. Aaron Lipovitz, the oldest of the Slipyer landsleit, is the president.

Another of the first anshei's to be founded was the Shomrei Shabbos congregation, formed in February 1909 as mentioned earlier.

The Shaarei Tzedec, founded on January 17, 1910, was the first congregation in Toronto organized by immigrants from Russia. The congregation began with seventeen members and its first president was Mr. Landsberg. It was first located on Edward Street, then on Centre Avenue, and today at 397 Markham Street. The Shaarei Tzedec has a membership of 150 and does not as yet boast a rabbi of its own. The president of the congregation at present is Mr. L. Eisen, who is also the president of the Toronto Mizrachi organization.

The large Roumanian congregation, Adath Yisroel Congregation, Men of Roumania was founded in 1903 and has a large synagogue of its own located on Bathurst Street. Rabbi Irwin Schilds, a recently arrived refugee from Germany, is its spiritual head, and Mr. N. Federman is its cantor. There is a membership of 200, with Mr. B. Donenfeld president and Mr. L. Caplan treasurer.

In 1910 a group of Roumanian immigrants organized another Roumanian congregation, the First Moldaver Congregation Tifereth Yisrael Anshei Roumania, and held services in a private home at 36 Edward Street. The initial membership was fourteen, with Mr. Eliezer Cohen the first president. The following members were present at the founding of this congregation: Mr. Moses Grouper, Mr. Joseph Moscovitz, Mr. Joseph Hershcovitz, Mr. J. Cohen, Mr. J. Solomon, Mr. I. Rosenthal, Mr. Ch. L. Rentzer, Mr. I. Tobias, Mr. M. Goldenthal, Mr. J. Altman, Mr. Mordechai Cohen and Mr. Joseph Magder. The majority of today's members are Roumanian born and they carry on as a landsmanschaft. The membership is seventy strong and the congregation has a shul of its own, at 267 Augusta Avenue, and a cantor, Mr. M. Goldenthal, but not yet a rabbi of its own. The president of the congregation is Mr. David Harris.

Ostrovtzer Shul Youth Orchestra, ca 1930
Conducted by Yeshua Yankel Barsh, centre, eminent violinist
who lived to be more than 100 years of age.

❧ The Ostrovtzer Shul (Cecil Street)

Forty years ago, about 1910, the Ostrovtzer Jews in Toronto organized a congregation called the Tifereth Yisroel Bikkur Cholim Anshei Ostrowze. The congregation started with fifty members and Mr. Lipe Silverman was its first president. The first Ostrovtzer Shul was on Teraulay Street, today's Bay Street. A couple of rooms were rented in the rear of the home of Lazar Berenstein, a Yivansker immigrant, and in these rooms, forty years ago, the foundations were laid for the present splendid edifice of the Ostrovtzer Synagogue.

The first years were difficult ones, with the congregation changing its quarters repeatedly. It moved from Teraulay Street to Elizabeth, from Elizabeth to St. Patrick Street, and from St. Patrick to Centre Avenue, where for the first time the congregation acquired a building of its own. The first president of the shul on Centre Avenue was Hershel Borkovsky, succeeded in office after a while by Elyahu Markowitz, the father of the prominent physician, Dr. Charles Markson.

Eventually a church on Cecil Street just east of Spadina Avenue was bought for $20,000 and remodeled into a synagogue. The full name of the great synagogue that now stands at 58 Cecil Street is Beth

Ostrovtzer Shul, Cecil & Spadina, ca 1950

Haknesseth Hagadol Anshei Ostrowse. Located in the centre of the Yiddish district in Toronto, the Ostrovtzer shul, with its handsome exterior is an important landmark and one of the sights to be pointed out to the Jewish visitor in Toronto. The synagogue was built through the efforts of many prominent Ostrovtzer landsleit. Its importance in the community today is the result of these efforts and of the devotion and large-hearted concern of the large membership. Particularly deserving of mention are Mr. Abraham Z. Linson, the first president and one of the most active members in the congregation, to whom credit goes for the modernization of the building; Mr. David Sussman, the present president of the synagogue; Mr. Israel Weinberg, president for more than twelve years; Mr. J. Rosenberg, the devoted secretary of the congregation for the past twenty-six years; and Mr. Isaac Gotlieb, the synagogue's treasurer. Others worthy of mention are past officers Mr. Louis J. Zuker, Mr. Abie Larenbaum and the brothers Abraham and Feivel Fidler. Mr. Louis J. Zucker, born and raised in Ostrowze, is a prominent Toronto barrister who has always been active in Ostrovtzer affairs. In addition to being executive chairman of the Canadian Federation of Polish Jews and president of the Yeshiva Torah Chayim, Mr. Zuker has served the Ostrovtzer Synagogue with great distinction, having been its president for several very fruitful years.

The Ostrovtzer Shul was founded for a three-fold purpose: it was meant to be a house of worship, a meeting place for landsleit, and a place where the poor and hungry could always find shelter. That it was the intention of the founders to provide aid to the needy can be seen in the fact that the congregation, in 1913, fully paid the hospital expenses of several of its members who had become gravely ill, and even provided money to send them back to Ostrowze. At present the Ostrovtzer Synagogue has a membership of about 200, but so far it has not yet acquired a rabbi of its own. For many years the Ostrovtzer shul has been a mecca for the leading cantors of the continent, many of whom have come again and again.

🕊 Chevra Shas & Rabbi Abraham Price

Among the anshei's we may also include the Chevra Shas, on Cecil Street. This congregation was founded in 1927 and is composed of immigrants from various small towns in Poland whose common interest is the study of the Torah. Their synagogue is less a house of worship than it is a house of study. Here the young student of religion and the pious elder scholar sit side by side pouring over the worn pages of the Talmud, chanting the ancient text in the traditional sing-song. In this congregation intellectual subtlety is more highly prized than rigidity of ritual and the members delight in unraveling the meaning of abstruse text in the Talmud or in throwing light on an obscure passage in one of the many commentaries on it.

Rabbi Abraham Price

The congregation Chevra Shas has a membership of about fifty. Its spiritual head is Rabbi Abraham Price. The first president was Mr. M. Rosenzweig and its present president is Mr. Abraham Biderman. Because of its reputation, well merited, as a center of rabbinical learning, the Chevra Shas exercises a greater influence in the religious life of the community than its small membership might suggest.

🕊 The Kiever Congregation

The Kiever shul was founded in 1912 and was originally called the Rodfei Shalom Anshei Kiev. According to Mr. B. Green, who came to Canada in 1907 and was one of the original members, the congregation was founded by a score of Ukrainian Jews who were members of the Russian Shul on Centre Avenue. The original members numbered twenty-six, of whom Mr. Leib Bassin and his two

Kiever Synagogue, Denison & Bellevue

brothers, Zisha and Motel, were the most active workers. The decision to found a new congregation was made in the home of the late Mr. Shloime Chomodelsky and the earliest services were held in his home at the corner of Elizabeth and Agnes (now Dundas) Streets.

During the First World War the congregation founded a Ukrainian Farband in the city to organize help for the Jewish population of Kiev and at the end of the war the members brought a number of orphaned Ukrainian children to Toronto. In 1927, Mr. Leib Bassin purchased a lot at the corner of Denison and Bellevue Avenue, and this site became the home of the Kiever shul. The membership of the shul has never exceeded twenty-six, and only during the High Holidays are large numbers of worshippers, consisting chiefly of people living in the neighbourhood, present. Mr. Litvak has been cantor of the shul during most of its life. It is worth mentioning that the majority of the members of this synagogue are engaged in the fruit business and in this respect the shul strongly resembles the "*chevra*" shul that used to flourish in the old country.

In 1927 a congregation called the Kehilath Jacob was founded with a membership of sixty-five. The location of this congregation is at 128 Markham Street. Owing to the great shift northward of the Jewish population the congregation's membership has declined to thirty-nine. Mr. I. M. Romanick is the congregation's present president.

The Polish Shul (*Beth Yakov*)

The largest of the anshei's in the city is the Polish shul, called the Beth Haknesseth Hagadol Beth Yakov.

Unlike the anshei's we have mentioned above, the Polish Shul had, from its very beginning, a heterogeneous membership composed of Jews who had come from widely separated localities in Poland. The congregation was officially founded in 1912, with an initial membership of sixty-five. A house was rented at 17 Elm Street and for several years the religious services were held in this section of the city, then the heart of the Jewish residential neighbourhood but now part of Toronto's downtown area. The Hassidic character of the shul attracted many members and when the congregation had become sufficiently large it was felt that the time had arrived to engage a rabbi. On the recommendation of his son-in-law, the congregation invited Rabbi Yudel Rosenberg to its pulpit. Rabbi Rosenberg, affectionately called Reb Yudel Tarler, was well known throughout Poland as a scholar, mystic and author and was eminently qualified for this position.

Rabbi Yudel Rosenberg was born in Skarshav, Poland, in 1860. In his early youth he was regarded as a prodigy, his precocious learning attracting wide attention. At the age of seventeen he married a girl from the town of Tarle and thereafter spent many years there studying the Talmud and other rabbinical literature. He received his *s'micha*, the rabbinical ordination, from three famous scholars: Rabbi Schneur Zalman (author of the famous *Tanya* and *Siddor Torah Or*); Rabbi Meir Yechiel Meltchek, the Ostrovtzer Rav; and Rabbi Zinvil Kleppish, one of the chief rabbis of Warsaw. Rabbi Yudel later became rabbi of Tarle, the home two centuries earlier of the celebrated "Pnei Yoshua," and remained there for several years, founding while he was there a yeshiva for advanced students.

Rabbi Yudel Y. Rosenberg

Beset by poverty and family misfortunes, and attacked by enemies in the town, Rabbi Rosenberg was forced to leave Tarle and begin a life of wandering. For a while he tried his hand at business but meeting with very little success he returned to his rabbinical calling. He journeyed from Lublin to Lodz and from Lodz to Warsaw, there to find a new position as a rabbi.

On receiving an invitation to head the local Polish congregation, Rabbi Rosenberg brought his family over to Toronto. This was in 1913. In Toronto too the newly arrived rabbi underwent hardships. There were many times when his family was critically short of food. It is reported that in some of his sermons he severely criticized the type of immigrant who went to America and these sermons were none too pleasing to some of his listeners. His attempts to organize the religious life of the community to introduce, for instance, the supervision of local kashruth, were at the time,

Hassidic Wedding on Steps of Henry Street Synagogue, 1928
The Twersky–Langner marriage was conducted under the "chupah" (canopy) outside Beth Jacob, the "Poylisher" shul on Henry Street. Illustration below by Aba Bayefsky.

alas, premature. Rabbi Rosenberg was deeply interested in education and was largely instrumental in founding the Talmud Torah Eitz Chaim which he headed for several years. He was the author of many scholarly works, one an excellent translation of the Zohar from Aramaic into Hebrew. But Rabbi Rosenberg lacked the wholehearted support of the community, although he had individual admirers in plenty. Consequently in 1917 he left for Montreal. In Montreal he fared much better than in Toronto, thriving there as a rabbi until his death in 1936.

In 1918 the cornerstone of the new Polish Shul, now called the Beth Jacob, was laid on its present site on Henry Street. The president of the new synagogue was Mr. Mendel Granatstein, head of the distinguished business and philanthropic family. Mr. Moishe Frimer and Mr. L. Zucker were among the earliest secretaries of the congregation. The congregation's president today is Mr. Kalman Silverstein and the well-known Berele Charloff is its cantor. The Beth Jacob has today no rabbi of its own, but on many occasions during the past two years it has had Rabbi Dr. David Ochs speak to the congregation.

The Polish Shul has always distinguished itself by its charity and by its generous contributions to Zionism and other worthy causes. In the synagogue's library there is an interesting letter from the Lubliner Rav, Rabbi Meir Shapiro (the founder of the famous Yeshiva Chochmei Lublin), warmly thanking the congregation for its generous help.

Recently the number of "anshei's" in the city has begun to decline. The membership is also declining. Most young people — the first and second generation children of the immigrants — do not feel the same attachment as their parents did to the landsleit congregations. The children of the immigrants are, instead, increasingly drawn to the societies and fraternal organizations that have sprung up in recent years. It is only parents that frequent the older anshei's, and they frequent them with the same enthusiasm as of old.

❧ Hassidic Congregations

In Toronto there are also a number of Hassidic *klausen* or *shtublach*, each *klaus* or *shtubel* composed of the followers of a different Hassidic rabbi. For example, there is the Beth Yisroel, which is the congregation of the Husiatener Hassidim. This congregation bears the name of the eminent

Leaflet Publicizing Husiatener Klaus Celebration, 1926
Husiatener Klaus Beth Israel held a community celebration of Simchas Torah in its building at 49 Ulster Street, corner Borden, in June 1926.

Husiatener–Tchortkover rabbi, Rabbi Israel Friedman, a direct descendant of the famed Rizhiner Rebbe, Yisroel'tche. In 1923 a group of his local disciples founded a congregation with Chaim Leib Stein, a shoichet, as its head. After repeatedly changing its quarters, the congregation finally acquired a building of its own at 96 Brunswick Avenue on the corner of Ulster Street. Today the congregation has a membership of more than 100, with many out-of-town Husiatener Hassidim among the members. Intensely pious, several minyanim of worshipper daily hold morning and evening services at this *shtubel* on Brunswick Avenue. Mishnayos and Gemara are studied nightly; Mr. Joseph Botnick, a prominent member of long standing, leads the study group in the Talmud. The Husiatener *shtubel* has often been a stop-over place for well-known Hassidic rabbis and Tsadikim passing through the city.

The late Rabbi Tsvi Kelman, a distinguished Talmudic scholar, was head of the congregation for many years. After his death he was succeeded by his son, the young Rabbi Abraham Kelman. Mr. Abraham Kurtz is president of the congregation today; lawyer Aaron Botnik, vice-president, and Mr. Sender Babbit, secretary.

Among the Hassidic congregations there are also the Beth Hamedrash of the Strettiner Rabbi, the Narayever Shul, and the Kiever Synagogue. The two latter synagogues were headed by sons of the Strettiner Rabbi. The Narayever Shul was founded in May 1914, with a membership of thirteen. According to its secretary, Mr. Moshe Haber, the congregation originally sought to organize its own sick benefit society but was unable to obtain a charter from the government because it had too few members. The congregation was originally housed at 142 William Street (today's St. Patrick Street), then at 70 Huron Street where it remained for more than twenty years; and finally acquired a permanent building at 187 Brunswick Avenue. Twenty-five years ago the congregation invited Rabbi Shloime Langner, the son of Rabbi Moshe Langner, the local Strettiner Rabbi, to be its spiritual leader. Mr. I. Ch. Katz was the congregation's first president and Mr. Mordechai Wasser is its president today. The membership of the Narayever Shul has grown from thirteen to seventy-five, and Rabbi Langner is still associated with the congregation.

Shaw Street Shul (B'nei Yisroel)

As the Jewish population in Toronto grew and spread out to newer neighbourhoods, it became increasingly difficult for many who wished to attend the older congregations to do so, their new homes being too far away. Consequently new congregations sprang up in these districts, their appeal being chiefly to people living in the neighbourhood.

In 1913, a congregation called the Chevra B'nei Yisroel was founded by a few people who held religious services in a rented house on Ossington Avenue. Mr. A. Wilson, a Lithuanian immigrant, was the first president, and Mr. Sh. Forman, a well-known children's teacher, was the first secretary. This small congregation was the foundation of the present large and spacious shul standing on the east side of Shaw

B'nai Israel — the Shaw Street Shul

The synagogue was designed by Kaplan & Sprachman and built ca 1929 on Shaw below Dundas, overlooking Bellwoods Park. Group photo, top, shows sanctuary ca 1950.

Street, just below Dundas. The membership is a mixed one, consisting of immigrants of Polish, Russian and Lithuanian origin. Sermons are often preached there by visiting rabbis, the synagogue being without a rabbi of its own.

For almost thirty years, Mr. Sh. Forman led several study groups, instructing the congregation's members in the Bible and the Talmud. In recognition of his long service he was recently presented with a diploma signed by Mr. Grainer expressing the congregation's warm appreciation.

The Shaw Street Shul has been particularly active in raising funds for Israel. Recently the congregation organized a society to make loans to any member needing financial help. The synagogue's present membership is 180. Its officers are: Mr. J. Shulman, president; Mr. M. Turnofsky, vice-president; Mr. N. Koppel, secretary. Mr. Koppel, a teacher by profession, sees to it that the shul adheres to the Orthodox line of its founders. The synagogue has had several outstanding cantors in the past. Its present one is Cantor A. Kalmus. Mr. Moishe Arnoff was the *shammus* or sexton for many years.

The Yavneh Congregation

There is also in Toronto a Zionist synagogue called the Yavneh Congregation. Founded in 1905, seven years after the founding of the Canadian Zionist Organization, the Yavneh Congregation has played an important role in propagating Zionism among the local Orthodox Jews. The congregation started with a membership of fifty under the leadership of Mr. M. Wolfson, the father of the prominent Toronto physician, Dr. Wolfson.

The synagogue was originally housed in the Zionist Institute, moving when the institute moved, first from Simcoe Street to Beverley Street, where it was located for many years, then to the Zionist Building at 651 Spadina Avenue, where it is now. The membership at present is 150 and the congregation gets along, like so many other congregations, without a rabbi of its own. The late beloved and popular Mr. Alexander Cash was one of the founders of this congregation; Mr. I. Gangbar, a prominent Toronto Zionist, is president; and Mr. I. Green, formerly a president for six years, is one of its most active members. All moneys raised in the shul are turned over to the Jewish National Fund.

Beth Yehuda

In 1923 a new congregation called the Beth Yehuda was formed on Ossington Avenue. The congregation started with fifteen members with Mr. Yehuda Levinson as president. The present location of the synagogue is on Dovercourt Road and the membership has grown to 210. In 1940, on the initiative of Mr. D. Joseph, a Talmud Torah, affiliated with the Associated Hebrew Free Schools, was opened in the synagogue, starting with twenty-two pupils. The present enrolment in the Talmud Torah is 190 but the school is no longer affiliated with the Brunswick Avenue Talmud Torah, being run independently by the Beth Yehuda shul under the supervision of Rabbi Abraham Kelman. Mr. M. Goldenberg is president of the synagogue and Mr. David Green is its cantor.

Agudath Yisroel Anshei Sefarad (Palmerston Avenue)

Two more synagogues worthy of mention are the Agudath Yisroel Anshei Sefarad and the Beth Jacob Congregation. The first, located at 151 Palmerston Avenue, was founded in 1914 with an initial membership of forty-five. Mr. K. Atkin was the first president and Rabbi Zvi Levy the first rabbi. Today the membership of the Agudath Yisroel is 120 and the congregation takes a very active part in charitable and philanthropic affairs. The shul has a ladies auxiliary and a sick benefit society, both of which are constantly raising funds for Israel and other causes. The present president of the synagogue is Mr. J. Cohen who has been an active and devoted member for many years. The Agudath Yisroel has no rabbi of its own.

Beach Hebrew Institute

The other synagogue, the Beth Jacob, is located on Kenilworth Avenue and is popularly called the Beach Hebrew Institute. This congregation was founded in 1918 and its services were at first held in a private house in the east end of the city. The present building of the congregation was acquired in 1919, the late Rabbi Jacob Gordon delivering the inaugural address. Mr. Mendel Gebirtig was the first president and Mr. Hillel Weinberg the first secretary. The late Mr. Benzion Nathanson, one of the pioneers of Canadian Zionism, was a prominent member of the congregation, acting

Shaarei Shomayim on St. Clair Avenue
At left, early drawing by Kaplan & Sprachman. Construction began in 1936 and the congregation worshipped in the basement until the sanctuary was completed in 1948.

as its *baal tefillah* (leader of prayers) for many years. For a long time the synagogue had a Talmud Torah of its own — the only one in the east end of the city — with a professional teacher at its head; but in 1946, because of large numbers of Jews leaving the east end for other sections, it became necessary to close the school.

Shaarei Shomayim Congregation

In the late Twenties the Jews of Toronto for the first time began to move in some numbers to the northern districts of the city, chiefly settling in the neighbourhood around St. Clair Avenue West. It was necessary at first for the religious element among the new residents to travel long distances in order to reach the nearest synagogues, most of them located in the center of the city south of Bloor Street. In 1929 fifteen men banded together to form the Brothers of Jacob Congregation and established the first synagogue in the northwest section of the city, at 73 McKay Street. The first elected officers of the congregation were: Mr. L. Clavir, president, Mr. J. Kronick, vice-president, Mr. O. Kling, treasurer, and Mr. A. A. Goldenberg, secretary. The congregation grew rapidly and sought larger quarters for the growing membership. Because of friction among the members a number of them withdrew from the Brothers of Jacob forming a congregation of their own which they called the Hillcrest Congregation. The present Shaarei Shomayim Synagogue on St. Clair Avenue is the direct successor of this congregation which was first founded in 1931. Some of the founding members of the Hillcrest congregation were Mr. J. Kronick, Mr. J. Andrews, Mr. A. Jacobson, Mr. M. H. Keyfetz, and Mr. G. Garfunkel.

For several years the High Holiday services were held at the St. Clair Robina Hall and in 1933 they were conducted in the Christie Street Talmud

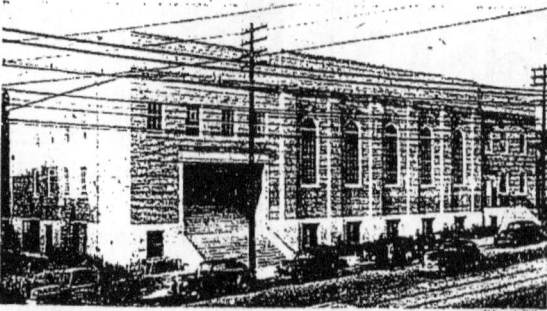

Opening of Shaarei Shomayim in Globe & Mail, Oct. 1, 1948
The story related that the building cost $500,000 and featured a unique memorial window believed to be the first in the world to depict the birth of Israel.

Torah. In 1934 the name of the Hillcrest Congregation was officially changed to Shaarei Shomayim. The congregation next sought to purchase the site of the Talmud Torah building but dropped the plan after the city authorities refused to grant a building permit. The lot on St. Clair Avenue where the building is now located was purchased for $5,525 and work was immediately begun. By the fall of 1936, the basement of the new synagogue had been completed and services were held there during the High Holidays of that year. When the number of worshippers reached almost one thousand the basement proved entirely inadequate. A campaign for funds to build the upper structure of the synagogue was launched in 1943, meeting with great success. In 1944 the congregation invited Rabbi Dr. Judah Washer of New Kensington, Penn., to occupy its pulpit and he has since remained the spiritual head of the Shaarei Shomayim. Dr. Washer is a past president of the Tri-State Zionist Region of the Zionist Organization of America, a member of the board of the United Jewish Welfare Fund of Toronto, a member of the board of the Canadian Jewish Congress (Central Region) and of the Associated Talmud Torahs of Toronto. Among the many offices he holds is that of member of the National Praesidium of the Mizrachi Organization of Canada.

The large auditorium of the new Shaarei Shomayim Synagogue was first used for religious services on Friday November 25, 1948, with Leibele Waldman of New York City as guest cantor. On Sunday November 27, the formal dedication of the synagogue took place and the ceremony was attended by the Hon. Roy Lawson, Lieutenant-Governor of Ontario, the Hon. Leslie Frost, Premier of Ontario, His Worship Hiram McCallum, Mayor of Toronto, and other distinguished guests. The new synagogue, the largest Jewish Orthodox congregation in Toronto, is located on St. Clair Avenue West between Atlas Avenue and Winona Drive, and has a seating capacity of 1,036. The synagogue includes a spacious auditorium on the main floor, a Holy Ark built of black Italian marble, a daily chapel in the basement, a young peoples' auditorium upstairs and facilities for a large library. An outstanding feature of the new building is the full-length stained glass windows in the auditorium of the synagogue, which depict stories from the Bible and scenes of modern Israel.

The Shaarei Shomayim is the first large synagogue in Toronto to make provision for the systematic education of the members' children, establishing a separate building for Talmud Torah on the same premises. This Talmud Torah too, like the synagogue of which it is now a part, has grown rapidly from humble beginnings. The first Talmud Torah in the north part of the city was established on Christie Street and after being briefly administered by Mr. Frank, a Hebrew teacher, the school was taken over by Rabbi Gringorten. Under his direction, the registration of pupils increased rapidly, and with the rising enrolment the Christie Street quarters became cramped and unsatisfactory.

In 1936 when the "hall" of the present Shaarei Shomayim Congregation was completed, the Christie Street Talmud Torah was moved there temporarily. At the same time, a Sunday School founded by the synagogue and headed by Mr. Jack Gringorten was organized, attracting many new pupils. In 1940 the Talmud Torah was incorporated into the Associated Hebrew Free Schools. The school building supplied by the congregation was formally opened in the fall of 1947, and is modern and spacious with the latest equipment and facilities. Today the Talmud Torah has eight classrooms and an enrolment of more than 400 children. The school has also initiated daily nursery and kindergarten classes. The principal of the Talmud Torah is Mr. Jack Burke, a graduate of the University of Toronto as well as a fine Hebrew scholar who received his pedagogical experience in the Brunswick Avenue Talmud Torah.

Built at a cost of $500,000 with the money chiefly raised through subscriptions from the members, the Shaarei Shomayim Synagogue is a monument to the devotion and energy of the congregation. It is hard to believe that only twenty years ago the members used to hold their services in rooms over stores or in rented houses, and that from a handful of members in 1931 the membership has increased to more than 500 today.

The officers of the congregation are: Mr. Louis N. Nadler, president; Mr. M. Garfinkel and Mr. Meyer W. Gasner, vice-presidents; Mr. Isadore Caplan, treasurer; Mr. Charles Anthony, secretary; Mr. Gershon Naftolin, gabbai; Mr. B. W. Goldenberg, parnos. Trustees are Messrs. S. Forcht, I. Gold, A. Jacobson, J. Lepofsky, and W. Samuel.

➣ Beth Sholom Synagogue

During recent years large number of Jews moved into Cedarvale and Forest Hill — northern suburbs of the city — and for a long time the more Orthodox Jews living in this section lacked a place of worship. But in January 1946 eighteen persons headed by Mr. Shore banded together and formed a congregation. The growth of this northern congregation has been phenomenal, with large numbers of new members joining eagerly. Recently a site for a new synagogue was purchased at the corner of Eglinton Avenue and Winnett Street and construction is now under way. When complete, the new Beth Sholom Synagogue will be the largest and most modern Orthodox synagogue in Toronto and its suburbs. The guiding spirit behind the undertaking is the synagogue's dynamic rabbi, Rabbi David Monson,

Beth Sholom
Above, artist's depiction of the new synagogue on Eglinton at Winnett.

At right, wartime military chaplain Rabbi David Monson (in uniform) stands with British Chief Rabbi Dr. Joseph Herman Hertz.

formerly rabbi of the St. Clair Avenue (Shaarei Shomayim) shul.

Rabbi Monson has given all his energies and talent to the planning and organizing of this synagogue and when built it will be a monument to his tremendous drive and vitality. The Beth Sholom is fast becoming a great religious and social centre for the Jewish residents of Cedarvale and Forest Hill. The synagogue already has a Talmud Torah of its own, affiliated with the Associated Hebrew Free Schools. Recently, too, a Sunday school was started and it is attracting many pupils. Qualified teachers have been engaged and the children are taught Jewish subjects in a warmly traditional atmosphere. The congregation now has a membership of more than 500.

Striking Women Garment Workers and Supporters, 1912
Their strike against the T. Eaton Company was long and bitter.

⁂ 5 ⁂

Jews in the
Needle Trades

WHEN WE BEGIN LOOKING at the origins of what is popularly considered to be the Jewish "needle trade" in the city of Toronto, we are at once struck by the unique manner in which it all began. The circumstances surrounding the rise of the Jewish manufacturer in the Toronto clothing industry are singular — and characteristically Jewish. In the case of the Jewish pioneers, the development of the garment industry followed a different trajectory from that which it usually does in the case of non-Jewish founders of an industry. Generally speaking, a new industry is started by people with large capital investing a considerable sum in a new enterprise. Through this large capital investment on the part of the owners a factory is built, equipment is acquired, workers are hired, and production finally started. The aim of the investor is large profits; that of the worker a decent livelihood. From the very first there is a clash of interests between the factory owners and employees. The manufacturer tries to keep production costs down, with wages at a minimum. To obtain a living wage and decent working conditions, the worker has to join with other workers in organizing a union to defend their common interests and rights. Thus under our system of private enterprise, the class divisions between employer and worker and between management and labour are, from the very first, decidedly marked.

Among the Jews of Toronto the process was different. The Jewish worker was the first to enter the clothing industry, the Jewish manufacturer following later. The latter did not come into the industry from outside the trade, bringing capital only. On the contrary, in the early 1900s the Jewish manufacturer came from within the garment trade itself, graduating from the work bench — from the cutting table or the sewing machine, sometimes even from the union's ranks. Thus, when the writer of this study interviewed manufacturers and union leaders, he found that their views regarding the clothing industry's early history largely coincided. The tales of early hardships were always the same, the accounts of early experiences always alike.

This circumstance accounts for the narrowness of the mental gulf separating the Jewish worker from his employer. How often one hears of the needle worker who slaps his employer on the back, points an admonishing finger at him and cries: "Don't be so uppity, I can still remember the day when you were one of us — an exploited worker!" The relationship between the Jewish worker and his employer is almost on a personal basis, with, quite often, almost no social barrier between them.

In considering the Jewish role in the growth of the needle trade it would be wrong to assume that this term — needle trade — applies only to the people engaged in the manufacture of wearing apparel. Actually, the needle trade embraces knitwear, embroidery, millinery, cap-making and the manufacture of pocket books and leather goods. The Jewish worker and manufacturer have shown as much ingenuity and resourcefulness in developing these related trades as they have in developing the men's and women's garment industries. The quality of the workmanship in these related trades, the styles, the fine materials used, and the attractive prices all attest to the high standards aimed at by those who engage in their production and manufacture. The enterprising Jewish businessman could always find a place for himself in the needle industry, his success or failure in the trade depending largely on his individual ability. Today the needle trades may be regarded as a field of activity predominantly Jewish.

Role of the Hebrew Journal

In writing the story of the development of this distinctly Jewish industry in Toronto, we must not ignore the great role played in the past forty years by the Toronto *Hebrew Journal* as a mediator in the frequent disputes between capital and labour. The pages of the *Hebrew Journal* mirror the turbulent life of the Toronto Jewish population during the first few decades of the century — which saw the emergence for the first time of an organized Jewish community life, the formation of the first Jewish unions, the appearance on the industrial scene of the small Jewish manufacturer. Many of the happenings then recorded in the columns of the *Hebrew Journal* might evoke a smile on the part of the reader today, while others would excite our sympathy: the struggle, for example, of the workers to unionize the shops, the difficulties facing the small Jewish businessman, the problems confronting the immigrant trying to adjust himself to local conditions.

It is virtually impossible today to obtain a clear picture of the founding of the garment trade in Toronto, or to capture the flavour of its colourful beginnings on Spadina Avenue (the garment centre of Toronto) without having constantly to refer to the back issues of the *Hebrew Journal*. At every turn the *Hebrew Journal* mirrored the hard struggle of the factory worker to gain a livelihood, just as it mirrored the struggle of the small manufacturer to stay in business. The struggle on either side was not a pretty one, nor was it a struggle for high ideals; it was, as a matter fact, a battle for sheer survival, against sweatshop conditions on the one hand, and against fierce business competition on the other. A bad season or a general trade slump and the manufacturer was out of business, the worker out of a job.

It may be said that the Jewish needle industry was born at about the same time that the *Hebrew Journal* was founded. This early period was the "golden era" in the early life of the Jewish population of Toronto. It stretched from the days just before the outbreak of the First World War to the years immediately after. Up to 1910, Jewish affairs were still in a formless state, unorganized and unplanned. But by 1911 the organized Jewish community was beginning to take shape. The first steps in organizing the activities of the immigrant Jewish population were being taken. Institutions were founded and schools established; community leaders were coming to the fore. At this stage in the development of the Jewish community a need began to be felt for a newspaper in which the needs of the Yiddish-speaking section of the community could be voiced and its problems discussed. In 1911, in response to this need, the Toronto *Hebrew Journal* was founded and to this day it remains a powerful factor in the shaping of the thoughts and opinions of the local community.

Those were the days, too, when the immigrant youth, energetic and ambitious, and anxious to build a new life after being uprooted from their old home in Europe, were eager to adapt themselves to the new conditions under which they lived. Those were the days when the local cloakmakers' union was born; when former factory workers, with limited capital and in the most daring manner, first began to break into the field of manufacturing. It was during the decade 1910 to 1920 that Jewish manufacturers began to blossom forth and that the unions first became strong.

Jewish Manufacturers & Unions Blaze the Trail

There are some valuable lessons to be learned from a careful study of the industrial scene in Canada during the years following the Second World War. In the years 1945, 1946 and 1947, the Canadian economic scene was shaken by a series of labour upheavals — a series of strikes and a lining up of the opposing forces of capital and labour. The whole of Canadian industry was affected and the repercussions are still felt today. What lay behind those sudden upheavals? The answer is to be found in the nature of the demands made upon industry by Canadian labour. The demands were for higher wages, better working conditions, union recognition and job security — the very benefits the Jewish needle worker had fought for and secured thirty years before.

Thirty years after the Jewish worker in the garment industry had wrung these concessions from his employer, they were not yet acceded by the industry as a whole. It was only because the Jewish manufacturer and the Jewish unions had learned to look at things realistically, and reach out for workable compromises, that there was peace in the clothing industry (with the manufacturer and the union leader able to talk over their differences over the conference table) at a time when the rest of Canada was being torn by industrial strife. The Jewish worker, through his early struggles for better conditions in the garment trade, had anticipated by fully thirty years the struggles of the Gentile fellow worker. Today, on the whole, the Jewish worker, through his unions, has achieved for his industry fair working conditions and a decent living standard. Thus the progressive Jewish manufacturer and the organized Jewish worker in the needle trades have together been pathfinders for harmonious relations between capital and labour in other industries.

It might be wise to explain what we mean by "Jewish industry," particularly when there are numerous Jewish businessmen associated with industries that cannot possibly be classified as Jewish. There are Jews, for instance, who are active in certain heavy industries such as lumber, oil, paper and coal. Until comparatively recent times there were no Jews engaged in these industries and they were almost exclusively Gentile. Nevertheless, despite the fact that some Jews have now entered these fields, we do not regard the industries as Jewish, since the role of our co-religionists in them is minor and the number of Jewish workers employed by them insignificant. Nor do we include the Jewish retail merchant, the professional man, the white-collar worker, nor even the small independent businessman in the trades that we categorize as specifically Jewish. Although these latter categories represent an important branch of the economic life of the Toronto Jewish community, they do not come under the heading of our present survey. Under the term "Jewish industry" we mean specifically the garment industry and the allied trades where the factories are Jewish-owned and the workers predominantly Jewish.

The Cloak Trade

The cloak trade may rightly be considered the parent trade of Jewish industry in Toronto. The manufacture of cloaks (women's coats and suits) was the "first swallow" heralding Jewish participation in the needle trades. The manufacture of cloaks was followed successively by the rise of the men's clothing trade, the fur trade, the millinery, embroidery, cap-making, pocket-book making, shoe manufacturing and finally, sportswear trades.

Joint Board Cloak, Skirt & Dressmakers Union, Toronto, ca 1918
Top row: A. Kirzner (left), Ch. Edwards, H. Kruger, T. E. Black, M. Shur, S. Koldofsky, M. Yampolsky. Middle: H. Konikoff, B. Seligman, E. Wilner, J. Sporn, J. Kosatchkoff, H. Wilner, H. Friedman. Front: Ch. Surber, M. Samuels, H. Anin, J. Franklyn, M. Fox, M. Weintraub, Jack Sheinkman.

But the beginning was made in cloaks. To obtain a better picture of the rise of the first Jewish trade in Toronto, we interviewed some of the pioneers of the industry — notably, the "old timers" who were present at the birth of the industry some forty years ago. As mentioned earlier, we got very similar stories from the manufacturer and the union organizer. The story of the "summer birds of passage," as told by Mr. Abraham Kirzner, is characteristic. Mr. Kirzner belongs to the older Jewish residents of Toronto; he was a pioneer labour leader for many years, an organizer for the International Ladies Garment Workers Union.

Who were the "summer birds of passage"? According to Mr. Kirzner they were experienced American Jewish tailors, mostly designers and cutters, who came to Toronto chiefly from Rochester and New York during the hot summer months when their trades were slack at home. This happened in the years 1908 to 1910 when, as mentioned above, the clothing trade was still largely under non-Jewish ownership. The Toronto factories were glad to get experienced tailors even for the short summer season and hired the American Jews with celerity; and after the season was over the latter would return home with their pockets well lined.

It was these Americans who introduced the idea of unionism to their Canadian fellow workers. In New York City, then the garment centre of the United States, the Jewish workers who predominated in the needle trades had begun to fight the sweatshop system with its long hours and its low pay; had started the great modern battle for more humane conditions. During the New York labour conflicts of 1910, masses of workers were fired from their jobs and great and embittered strikes followed. Similar strikes, on a small scale, also took place in Toronto. Owing to these Toronto strikes and also because of anti-union discrimination, many Toronto needle workers were jobless and some adventurous spirits among them seized on the idea of setting up as manufacturers on a small scale as a means of making a living.

The manner of setting up in business was as follows. An operator or a cutter would rent a couple of rooms or an attic flat, move in a sewing machine or two, hire a couple of operators and start making clothes. The new employer would work alongside his employees, slave like them at the machine, cut the material himself, sort out the garments, and then try to dispose of his finished goods to the highest bidder. He would work long hours and would often forego his wages at the end of the week, living frugally from hand to mouth. The upstart manufacturer knew that he could only stay in business if he met the prices of his competitors and that only his skill, the quality of the work he turned out, and the lowest possible production costs would enable him to get by. Most of the small Jewish manufacturers in Toronto started in business this way, working hard and contenting themselves with meagre profits in the hope of establishing themselves eventually on a firm footing. This was the way of the pioneer, and this was true not only in cloaks but also in every other branch of the needle trades.

The first steps taken by the new manufacturer were timid and uncertain, like the first steps of a child learning to walk. It is at this stage of the growth of the industry that we first encounter the contractor. The contractor was a hybrid creature, "half boss, half worker." He worked longer and harder than his employee, often enlisting the aid of his wife and children and sometimes even of his mother-in-law. All slaved together under the most difficult conditions, suffering many hardships, until with a little success they would at last be able to stand firmly on their feet.

Many of the first contractors, especially those in the men's clothing trade, came from outside the trade proper, not having before worked in tailoring shops. This is how it usually came about. A peddler, after years of knocking on doors, would manage through scrimping and saving to accumulate a little capital. This he would invest in a few sewing machines and some bolts of material. Knowing nothing of the trade, he would work at home together with his family, and then sell the finished garments to the Gentile wholesaler. In a short time he would blossom out as a "contractor," hiring extra workers to increase production. Many of the Jewish manufacturers and wholesalers now prominent in the garment industry originally started as contractors. Indeed, contracting was usually the first rung in the ladder of advancement for the manufacturing pioneers in the clothing industry.

From Tailor Shop to Professional

An unusual type of garment worker was the young immigrant who would work as an operator or presser in a clothing factory, then quit his job after saving up some money in order to go to the university. Many of today's prominent members of the community started their professional careers in this way. They had been burningly ambitious young men panting for a higher education and anxious for careers in medicine, law, pharmacy and other professional fields. It was not merely ambition to better themselves financially that they had; they were, one and all, possessed of a deep and genuine hunger for knowledge. If the lot of the average Jewish worker was hard in those years, that of the student, working by day and studying by night, was, as can be imagined, definitely tougher.

To begin with these students usually came from homes so poor that their wages were needed to help out with the rent and food. It was impossible for them to depend financially on their parents. Consequently they were forced to find part-time work either by day or in the evenings. They worked in factories during the summer months and whatever money they would earn over and above their school needs they would hand over to their families. The unions resented these young part-time workers and placed special difficulties in their way.

Under such circumstances did many of the early professional workers live in those early days. A few of the men now prominent in the community who started this way are Dr. David Pearlman, Mr. M. Schwartz, the late Dr. J. L. Solway, Dr. J. L. Hamil (Kimelstein) and Dr. Nathan Rosen.

Dr. Hamil has described for us the problems confronting the young students in those days. "Those were truly exciting days," he said, wrinkling his forehead reflectively as he recalled the life of that bygone period. "The Jewish community was alive with factions and teemed with idealistic groups and youth organizations, each dreaming of some utopia of its own. Making money was scarcely thought of — no one cared very much about making a large fortune. Every Jewish home was a cosy haven for the lonely immigrant; everyone was ready to share everything with his friends and neighbours and looked forward to the day, not far off, when socialism would dawn to free mankind of drudgery."

The Cloakmakers Union

The Toronto Cloakmakers Union was organized in 1911. Previous to that there had been only one union in the local garment industry, a branch of the international union organized by the Industrial Workers of the World. The branch, known as the IWW Local, was established here in 1905 but failed to make much headway among the local clothing workers, the industry on the whole remaining unorganized until the advent of the Cloakmakers Union. During the time that the IWW union was active in the city, the Jewish population of Toronto numbered only 18,000 and the overwhelming majority of the garment workers were non-Jewish.

Just about this time, too, the Canadian government, anxious to build up the sparsely populated country, threw open its gates to immigration from abroad. Thousands of Jewish immigrants streamed into Canada, fleeing Czarist Russia for fear of reprisals against socialists and Jews after the attempted assassination of the Czar. Most of the newcomers were young; a few came from comfortable middle-class homes but the majority were workers unable to scratch out a decent living in Russia and Poland.

Since many of the occupations these workers had been engaged in were uncommon in Canada, the immigrants were soon up against it financially. What occupations could they turn to? Some took to peddling, which required no previous training and which allowed them to have the Sabbath day off. Some became day labourers in the local iron and steel foundries, working long hours at jobs they were unaccustomed to and physically more or less unsuited for. Others, embittered at not being able to find work and suffering pangs of hunger, were induced to join missionary societies where at least they could get a meal and a bed.

So it was that in the early days, if a Jewish immigrant found a job in a Gentile clothing factory or tailoring shop, he regarded it as a great stroke of good fortune. He would try to get his friends in, and later his landsleit. Eventually most of the newcomers, regardless of their previous social or occupational backgrounds, were absorbed into the garment industry, accepting thankfully the long hours of work and the miserable wages that the trade offered.

In the early years of the New York garment industry there existed what was known as "season unions," workers' associations that sprang up in the clothing district whenever work was plentiful only to vanish as soon as the season was over. This, however, was not the case with the Industrial Workers of the World, a militant labour organization that exerted a powerful influence on the American labour movement. At the height of its influence the IWW had numerous branches all over the United States and Canada, but when for reasons too complicated to be discussed here its power began to wane, many of its branches disappeared, the Toronto IWW included. For a while there were no unions at all in the city of Toronto, the local manufacturers naturally welcoming this state of affairs and taking full advantage of the situation. Conditions in the clothing industry grew worse, wages fell, and the interests of the garment workers were not so much as thought of.

At this point we hear once again of the "summer birds of passage" mentioned before. A crisis in the clothing industry in the city of New York, with the collapse of the union there, caused some thirty American Jewish cutters and operators to move to Toronto and settle here. These men became the strong core of a new union, the International Ladies Garment Workers, formed in Toronto by workers determined to wrest better living conditions for themselves.

True, a local branch of the International Ladies Garment Workers Union, known as Local 48, ILGWU, had been formed in Toronto as early as 1907, but it did not become an important force in the industry until 1911 when these Americans began to make themselves felt. It is not our aim here to write the history of the cloakmakers union, but the story of its rise is so interesting a chapter in the history of the Toronto Jewish community that we were unable to refrain from sketching in an outline of its beginning. It is astonishing to see how humble was the start was of the present mighty and powerful ILGWU. We wish to pay our respects here to the founders and organizers of the union — the devoted workers who helped to mould its character and shape its future.

Some of the more outstanding leaders of the ILGWU during the past forty years have been the following: the late Mr. Joseph Cash, Mr. Nathan Cohen, Mr. S. Colofsky, Mr. Sam Galinsky, Mr. Abraham Kirzner, Mr. Dave Kreisman, Mr. Sam Kreisman, Mr. Chaim Langer, Mr. A. Megerman, Mr. Saul Poliakov, Mr. Yudel Rodjinsky, Mr. Benny Rotman, Mr. Bernard Schon, Mr. Charlie Shatz, Mr. Dave Tobias, Mr. Abie Weinstock, Mr. Wolinsky and Mr. Yampolsky. But the chief credit for building up the union must go to the rank and file membership, the ordinary union members without whose loyalty and devotion the union would never have achieved its present eminent position. Some of the union's founders are no longer living, others have left for new homes, but their work on behalf of the union will long be remembered and their names cherished.

The Neutral Chairman

The appointment of a neutral chairman to arbitrate conflicts in the garment industry marked an important step forward in needle trade affairs. Mr. Sam Kreisman, the present chairman of the Toronto local of the ILGWU and one of its most prominent leaders, is the source for the material about to be presented here. In his long association with the union, Mr. Kreisman has witnessed many far-reaching developments: recognition of the union as the representative of the workers, the acceptance on the part of the employers of the principle of the closed shop — but all and all Mr. Kreisman hails the appointment of a neutral chairman as perhaps the most important gain achieved by the union.

What is meant by the term "neutral chairman"? It means that if a disagreement develops between the employer and the union, with both sides refusing to budge from their positions and a compromise impossible, the matter is handed over to the neutral chairman for arbitration. The chairman is usually a respected member of the community, well informed about the problems of the industry, and with a reputation for fairness and honesty. Both sides agree in advance to accept his decision as binding.

Summer Dresses & Fall Hats from M. Pullan & Sons, ca 1910
The ads appeared in the Toronto Star in June 1910 and September 1911. Pullan's, a well-known ladies' wear store, was anchored on the city's main commercial boulevard in the heart of downtown.

Only after years of wrangling and arguing did this principle of neutral mediation receive general acceptance in industry, and it was not until fairly recently that it was adopted by the garment trade. The idea of outside arbitration to settle differences is of course not a new one. The principle is deeply rooted in Jewish history. It has always been a common practice for the two parties in a dispute to bring their case before the rabbi or some other disinterested third party. But the authority of the rabbi today is not what it used to be, especially in secular affairs, and he is seldom if ever asked to intervene in labour matters.

Today these ancient Jewish principles, with only slight modifications, are generally accepted in the western world and have become established in American industrial relations. It is possible to find in the Talmud authority for even the most recent innovation in management-labour relations introduced by the Department of Labour, namely the "cooling off period," a mandatory period of waiting during which employer and union are compelled by law to explore the possibilities for settling a dispute before resorting to a strike or a lockout.

Things were not quite so rosy in the field of industrial relations twenty years ago. The unsettled conditions in the needle trade during the years 1918 to 1934, the depression of 1920-21 and the accompanying unemployment, the periodic strikes in the industry climaxed by the general strike of 1934 — all this created bitter feeling between the manufacturer and the union. The atmosphere then was not propitious for the idea of mediation; suggestions for having a board of arbitration for the garment industry were considered impractical and premature. The manufacturer was hostile to the unions, considering their demands impudent, and the worker regarded his employer with suspicion and distrust. The office of neutral chairman was not created until the general strike of 1934 was settled, but since then it has been a most important force in the industry.

There have been two chairmen since the office was created — Mr. Samuel Kronick and Dr. Jacob Finkelman. Mr. Kronick is a prominent local businessman sympathetic to labour and with a well-deserved reputation for incorruptibility. Dr. Finkelman is a distinguished professor of law at the University of Toronto. Both men served with distinction and contributed greatly to the high esteem in which the garment industry is held in labour circles and in the community as a whole. Chiefly owing to the fairmindedness and impartiality of their decisions, the Jewish

Some 15,000 Torontonians marched in an anti-fascist rally on Spadina Avenue, July 1933.

labour stage, very stormy before, has stayed calm, with very little strife corroding relations between employers and unions.

The Rise of Hitlerism

It may sound paradoxical but the rise of Hitlerism in Germany in 1933 resulted in improved industrial relations in the cloak trade. The Jewish manufacturer and the Jewish worker both felt the senselessness of fighting each other at a time when they should be uniting their forces against the common enemy. Without formally discussing the matter they felt unconsciously that strife among themselves would only give aid and comfort to the destroyers of their people. They were loath at such a moment to divert the minds of the Canadian people from the Nazi evil through focusing attention upon fights among themselves. Voluntarily they decided to reduce friction between Jew and Jew and to seek to enlist the sympathy of the Gentile, worker and employer alike, against the threat posed by the Nazis. That the Jewish unions played a great role in awakening Canadian labour to the Nazi peril is indubitable. The same solidarity between employers and workers was again demonstrated at the end of the war when Jewish manufacturers and unions joined in a common project to bring survivors in the displaced persons camps to Canada.

The unions spoke out on behalf of immigration, influencing many of the larger Canadian unions to raise their voices in support. The friendly collaborative spirit existing between the Jewish employer and unionist will soon be demonstrated more concretely when the cloakmakers celebrate the fortieth anniversary of their organization. Undoubtedly many of the manufacturers will be invited to the celebration and they are certain to occupy conspicuous positions at the head table. For the manufacturer too has realized that the union is not an antagonist but a collaborator, that it has at heart the welfare of the industry as a whole, the welfare of the manufacturer included. The manufacturer and the worker realize at this time of day, that they both stand to profit by working together in practical harmony.

✒ Insights of a Leading Manufacturer

Mr. Abraham Rovner, for many years acting president of the Jewish Old Folks Home, is prominent in local Jewish affairs. He is one of Toronto's oldest cloak manufacturers — an outstanding and very respected figure in the ladies garment trade. Mr. Rovner started manufacturing more than thirty-five years ago when the industry was still, so to speak, in its teething stage and had as yet scarcely emerged from its swaddling clothes. Mr. Rovner grew up with the industry, rising to be president of the Manufacturers Association, which office he held for many years. Because of his wealth of knowledge of the industry, we approached Mr. Rovner for information. Some of the things he had to say are most illuminating.

Mr. Rovner told us, for instance, that there are now between seventy-five and eighty 'Jewish' cloak factories in Toronto, the overwhelming majority solidly unionized. He also threw considerable light on a subject, fascinating to a degree, about which there is very little factual material — namely, the changing attitudes of parents and children towards the tailoring trades. Generally speaking, Jewish children do not follow in the footsteps of their immigrant parents when it comes to choosing a profession. Canadian-born sons of immigrants strike out on their own; they usually scorn the occupations of their "greenhorn" fathers. And nine times out of ten it is the parents themselves who are responsible for their children's sentiments.

The educated person has always been held in high esteem in the Jewish community, and every Jewish parent has always pined to educate his children. Indeed, the Jewish parent often made great personal sacrifices for the sake of his children, toiling like a galley slave that his offspring might enter the professions and become a rabbi, doctor, lawyer, engineer. It was not so much a desire for prestige as a desire on the part of the parent to save his son from the hardships that he had himself endured. A Jewish operator or pants presser would sooner have wished to cut off his right arm than to see his son working in a garment factory. To send his son through college he was ready to mortgage his home and live in the most dire poverty. Admittedly, the choice of occupation open to the Jewish youth was not very wide, but at any rate, he would be able to be his own boss — that was the important thing.

It was therefore surprising to learn from Mr. Rovner that these tendencies, so strong before, are not so strong now, and that a most noteworthy change has set in. According to Mr. Rovner, many sons of clothing manufacturers, who a few years ago would have scorned to go into the clothing industry, are now associated in business with their parents. He mentioned a large number of Canadian-born young men who are now active in the needle trades, and pointed to numerous business firms who have "& Son" tacked on to their names: Saltzman & Son, for instance, Ginsberg & Son, and others. This revolutionary shift is proceeding so rapidly that there are cases of professional men abandoning their professions and going into the garment industry. We do not know whether this is an exclusively Jewish trend or not, but it is certainly worth drawing attention to as a most interesting development in the dynamics of Jewish life.

Unfortunately, all this does not hold true with regard to the children of the Jewish worker, very few of whom think as yet of going into the clothing trade. The number of Jews in the garment trade is, Mr. Sam Kreisman has told us, steadily falling. A few years ago the Jewish worker predominated in every branch of the industry; today, he plays an increasingly minor role. In the cloakmakers union, for instance, the membership was for a long time almost entirely Jewish, but now, out of a membership of 1,700, the Jewish workers form only 60% of the whole. Of the 1,100 workers in the dressmakers union, Jews are less than half; and of a total membership of 600 in the sportswear union, they constitute less than 6%. Thus, at the very time when the sons of the Jewish manufacturer are increasingly turning to the clothing trade, the sons of the worker are more and more turning to the other occupations.

In reply to our question whether there had been any noticeable improvement in employer–worker relations since the entrance of the manufacturers' children into the businesses of the parents, Mr. Kreisman tactfully said that "the apple does not fall far from the tree," and that if the father had been opposed to unions the son, educated or not, was likely to be so too. Nevertheless it is clear that the manufacturer today is giving more attention and consideration to the welfare of the worker.

The ladies garment worker enjoys many benefits today that he lacked only a short time ago. Through his union he has acquired a minimum wage scale, a forty-hour week, time and a half for overtime, two weeks vacation with pay, and a system of promotions and pensions. Perhaps the younger manufacturer has learned that a more sympathetic attitude to labour pays off in higher production and bigger profits.

Among the Jewish manufacturers and pioneer firms that started manufacturing more than forty years ago are the following: J. H. Winters & Company; Wilson & Waldman; Hutner Brothers; Goldstein & Jacobs; Sunshine Cloaks; Posluns Cloaks & Suits; Mr. Bregman of the Patricia Cloaks; Mr. Abraham Rovner of the Acme Cloak; Mr. Max Berman of the Aetna Cloaks; Mr. M. Frankfort, Mr. Rosenberg and Mr. A. Price.

Each manufacturer had to undergo many trials and overcome many obstacles. The story of Mr. Rovner is typical; his experiences mirror the struggles of the Jewish manufacturers. He was not one of the "summer birds of passage" described earlier — those Jewish workers who came to Toronto to make a little extra money during the summer months and then returned home in the fall. As an immigrant, he had landed in New York and had stayed there some time. He had found a job in a cloak factory and before long had become an experienced operator. In 1911 he came to Toronto to visit relatives and was so enchanted with the city that he decided to remain. He went to New York for his bride, was married in Toronto, and has been living here ever since. From the first Mr. Rovner was an enthusiastic union man, and soon after he started on his first job in Toronto — with M. Pullan & Sons — this enthusiasm of his was noticed and the small local union he belonged to appointed him shop chairman.

In those days the Jewish factory worker accepted his hard lot with an apathetic sort of fatalism. He was constantly haunted by the fear of incurring the wrath of his employer. The worker at the Pullan plant, for instance, regarded the privilege of being allowed to interrupt his work for the evening prayers as more important than that of joining a union, and then perhaps losing his job if found out. His take-home pay after a full week's work plus overtime usually amounted to little more than $15. Yet he was happy to get even that.

The secretary of the union at Pullan's at that time was Mr. Yampolsky. Mr. Berger was the shop chairman. When a strike broke out in the factory, more energy had to be spent by the union in keeping the workers from returning to work than in fighting the employers. Mr. Rovner relates a curious incident that took place during that strike. Pullan's decided to hire a gang of strike breakers in Montreal and bring them to Toronto by truck. The union learned of this and by a clever ruse foiled the company's attempt to smash the strike, forcing the firm to make a settlement of the union's terms. The ruse was of an unusual order. A number of Montreal union men hired themselves out as scabs, receiving handsome payment in advance. Then, when they arrived in Toronto and entered the shop, they started without much ado to smash the plant's machinery. The Pullan firm capitulated swiftly.

After leaving Pullan's Mr. Rovner started working at the Robert Simpson Company's garment factory. Wages and working conditions were better than before but the fierce competition from the large number of small Jewish factories springing up all over the city began cutting into the company's sales. Finally, in 1915, the Robert Simpson Company shut down its garment shop. Out of a job, Mr. Rovner began looking for a new occupation. Then, with a partner and joint capital of $800, he started the Just-Rite Cloak Company, beginning his meteoric rise in the cloak industry.

The abnormal wartime conditions created a heavy demand for clothes of every sort. Business boomed, profits soared, fortunes were made. After a business partnership lasting only twenty-two months, Mr. Rovner was able to pay off his partner nearly $100,000 for the latter's share in the business. Shortly afterwards he acquired the Acme Cloak Company of which firm he has remained head up to the present day. Mr. Rovner guided his firm through many slumps and business depressions, managing, often by his courage alone, to keep the firm going during the darkest days and winning in the end personal wealth and a prominent position in the business world.

The business career of Mr. Rovner, with its ups and downs and zigzag course, is typical of that of most early Jewish manufacturers. Former workers themselves, they always remembered their humble beginnings and were therefore inclined to regard their employees with a good deal of sympathy and understanding. This in large part accounts for the high standards and excellent employer-worker relations existing in the Toronto garment industry.

Dresses, Sportswear, Children's Wear

Three kindred manufacturing trades — dresses, sportswear, children's wear — are closely related to cloaks and together with cloaks now fall under the jurisdiction of the International Ladies Garment Workers Union. The proportion of Jewish manufacturers in these trades is just about the same as in cloaks, with dress manufacturers heading the list (there are seventy-five

Old-fashioned sweatshop

of them all told). Jewish workers are not nearly so numerous in them as in cloaks: there are but 40% in the dress trade and only 5% in the sportswear and children's wear trades.

Long before the workers in these kindred trades built their organization, the cloakmakers already had a strong and virile union. Conditions at first were chaotic in the dress, sportswear and children's wear industries, but with the help of the older union these trades too became well organized. Eventually the ILGWU negotiated a collective bargaining agreement with the association representing the manufacturers, obtaining the same benefits for the workers in the dress, sportswear and children's wear trades as for those in the cloak industry. Thus we see how unions originally organized for Yiddish-speaking clothing workers brought better working conditions and higher standards of pay to Gentile workers in allied needle trades.

The entrance of Jews into men's wear manufacturing also followed hard on the heels of their entrance into the manufacturing of ladies' cloaks. These two Jewish industries can really be said to have started at the same time, in the first decades of the century. The early men's wear manufacturers, like the cloak manufacturers, were almost all Russian Jewish immigrants who had come to Canada after the start of the Russo-Japanese war. The two industries had the same kind of birth pangs: success came only after long and difficult struggles. The unions had equally hard rows to hoe. The manufacturer, starting with a tiny capital and almost no equipment, had to compete with old established Gentile firms; the unions, in industries where sweatshop conditions were taken for granted, had to start from scratch — they first had to overcome the hostility of the workers to the idea of unionism, next had to educate the workers to some conception of their rights, and lastly had to weld them into an enthusiastic and highly disciplined body.

⇒ The Men's Wear Industry

At first when the manufacturing of men's wear was exclusively in the hands of Gentiles, the "greenhorn" Jewish immigrants needed a good deal of courage to set up as business competitors. Often risking the savings of a lifetime, sometimes using money borrowed from friends and relatives, the young immigrants would start on a shoestring and build up their enterprises slowly. They were always spurred on to success by the knowledge that failure would mean going back to a life of drudgery at the sewing machine or the cutting table.

Who were the first Jewish manufacturers of men's wear? We shall mention only a few of the more prominent names. There was Mr. Philip James who opened a business under the name Toronto Clothing, which today, greatly expanded, is called the James Brothers Company and is headed by his sons. There were Mr. Steinwortzvel, Mr. Zeidel and Mr. Leibel who organized the Bradford Woollens now known as Stone Clothing. There were Mr. Shatzky, Mr. Noble, Mr. Herman and Mr. Renzel who were clothing contractors before branching out into manufacturing. There was Mr. David Dunkelman who started Tip Top Tailors and the Gelber Brothers who founded the Imperial Clothing Company. Today, some of these pioneers head large nationally known firms and play important roles in the commercial life of the city.

Unlike the pioneers of the cloak trade, most of whom were ex-needle workers themselves, the first Jewish manufacturers of men's wear came from outside the industry — from peddling, real estate and other fields. The story of Mr. Sigmund Lubelsky, though somewhat unusual, illustrates the often accidental manner in which the Jewish manufacturers entered the men's wear industry. Mr. Lubelsky, a poor young immigrant was befriended by Mr. Frank Benjamin, a wealthy assimilated and socially established businessman who was then head of the metal firm Samuel and Benjamin. This firm is still prominent today. Incidentally, a son of this Mr.

Stereopticon View of Men's Cutting Room, T. Eaton Company, 1910
Eaton's freely hired Jewish tailors and tailoresses to work in its factories. In 1912 the union went on strike to protest against the company's attempts to introduce technological improvements in its factories.

Benjamin rose to be Brigadier General of the Jewish Brigade in the Second World War.

Mr. Benjamin was an ardent British patriot and it was his ambition to assist in the wider opening of the Canadian market to British textiles. With this in view he organized an importing business and worked hard to popularize British goods in this country. Impressed by the ability of the young Mr. Lubelsky, with whom he had become acquainted, Mr. Benjamin advanced him $800 to set up a business of his own, stipulating however, that all the materials Mr. Lubelsky purchased should be of British make. Off to a flying start by the leg-up given it by Mr. Benjamin, Mr. Lubelsky's firm prospered from the start.

❧ The Strike against Eaton's, 1912

In 1900 the T. Eaton Company, with the largest store in the British Empire and ranking first in the field of retail merchandising, opened a factory in Toronto and began manufacturing men's and ladies clothes. There was a heavy demand for ready-made clothing, and as the T. Eaton Company could not manufacture enough in its own factory to meet the demand, it farmed out unfinished garments to private contractors and private individuals for finishing.

With the large influx of Jewish immigrants into Canada after the turn of the century, many of them experienced tailors, there was a sharp increase

T. Eaton Company Store & Factories, Queen & Yonge Streets, 1920
Many Jewish tailors left Eaton's after the 1912 strike and set up shops of their own, thus giving rise to the Spadina "shmattah" industry. Below, two employment ads, dated 1907 (left) and 1916.
Opposite: View of Eaton's factory, 1921

YOUNG WOMEN WANTED

BY

T. EATON CO. LIMITED

We are constantly adding to our whitewear manufacturing plant the latest high-speed type of sewing machines, and we are open at all times to engage experienced operators on waists, underwear, etc. The work is strictly high-class, the pay excellent, and employment constant throughout the year. We also have in connection with these departments schools for instructions, so that beginners may quickly learn to operate electric power machines and earn good salaries.

To the beginners we give good wages right from the start, and have experienced people to give them instruction without charge.

Applications received all day long at our

EMPLOYMENT BUREAU,
12 Albert Street.

WANTED

BY

T. EATON CO. LIMITED

EXPERIENCED
OPERATORS ON
CLOAKS and SKIRTS

ALSO

HAND SEWERS
AND FINISHERS

APPLY

FACTORY
EMPLOYMENT OFFICE
16 LOUISA STREET.

in the number of Jews working for the company. Eaton's was anxious to increase its production, and hired almost anybody with some experience in tailoring. At first many immigrants, when applying for a job, gave their origin as German, believing that they would be taken on more quickly if their Jewish ancestry was unknown. But the T. Eaton Company, as a matter of fact, did not practice discrimination in hiring factory hands. At one time or another, during the early years of the present century, most Jewish tailors here had worked for the T. Eaton Company, and for many years Jews formed an impressive part of the personnel in its factory.

Several Jewish pioneers furnished us with valuable information regarding the beginnings of the men's wear industry in Toronto. Mr. David Stein, long an active leader of the local union, was especially helpful. He gave us a vivid, rounded picture of the early days in the trade. We shall confine ourselves here to retelling his story of the strike that broke out almost forty years ago in the clothing factory of the T. Eaton Company. Although originally called by the cloakmakers union, the strike had immediate repercussions in the men's wear trade.

Employees were paid by the piece-work system and it was a rule that a worker in the factory must earn no less than $5 a week if single and $7.50 a week if married. Naturally a slow or incompetent worker who could not earn this minimum would not stay long on the job. The firm was strongly opposed to unionism and forbade any form of union organization among its employees. It refused to recognize official labour holidays. An employee who absented himself on such a day was more likely than not to be fired when he showed up the next day.

Nevertheless the Jewish workers formed a union, and in 1912, when factory conditions were particularly hard, they went out on strike. Under the leadership of the United Garment Workers Union, which then had its headquarters in a shabby downtown office on Elizabeth Street, the men's tailors struck in sympathy with the cloakmakers, joining them in a long-drawn-out and costly affair.

This strike is in some ways unique in the history of the local needle trades. When we examine the circumstances that brought it about we are struck by the naivete, by the innocent idealism, of the early unionists, who were willing to endure heavy sacrifices for the sake of an idea that is today thoroughly outmoded.

What was the cause of the strike? It may sound incredible but it was called to protest against the attempts of the T. Eaton Company to introduce technological improvements in its factory. The immediate cause was a new machine installed by the firm — a machine for sewing linings on undergarments. Before this machine was invented linings had to be sewn on by hand, but with the new invention the work could be done faster and cheaper. For the needle worker this seemed a disaster; it spelt unemployment, hunger, charity. The Jewish garment worker saw in the machine a threat to his job and his security. Except that they were on a much smaller scale the issues here were those that agitated the English working-classes a century before when the industrial revolution was just under way. Now, as then, the machine was feared, resented and fought.

Although the strike had, from the very first, little chance of success — the union was too weak to wage a successful fight against so wealthy a firm — the workers carried on a hard and heroic struggle. The whole Jewish population rallied behind the strikers. Out of sympathy with them Jewish housewives organized a boycott of the firm's stores, refusing to buy goods there until a settlement was reached. Mr. Stein mentioned the street parades that the unions held in order to acquaint the public with the strikers' grievances and demands; he spoke of the daily arrests of strikers, of soldiers being called out to disperse them along with their sympathizers, of the T. Eaton Company's bringing in a shipload of strikebreakers from England, of men who were strikers one day and scabs the next, and of the clashes that occurred between Jewish strikers and Jewish strikebreakers.

Despite all efforts of workers and union, the strike was lost after fifteen bitter weeks. Its disastrous outcome was a crushing blow to the union, but the issue could not have ended otherwise. On one side was the union, small, weak, and without funds: at the outbreak of the strike there was only $200 in its treasury. On the other side was the T. Eaton Company — a mighty business concern, strong, influential, wealthy.

The effects of the defeat were felt for a long time in the entire garment industry. Jewish labour organization in the city was shattered, the unions were financially ruined, and the men's tailors were plunged into hopelessness and apathy. The T. Eaton Company now introduced a policy of quiet discrimination against Jewish workers, refusing to take back any of the former strikers. With diminished opportunities for work and a dread of having to go job hunting, some of the more ambitious and enterprising workers tried, like others before them in cloaks, to go into business on their own hook.

It is interesting to note that many of the future Jewish cloak manufacturers of Toronto took part in this strike either as strikers or strikebreakers. Two of the most active figures in the union at the time were Mr. Lubelsky, a designer in charge of organizing the cloaks section, and Mr. Harry Waksman, who looked after the men's wear. A few of the leaders of this strike in 1912 were Messrs. Max Shore, Abraham Nissenwater, Abraham Kirzner, B. Wilkowsky, Max Finkelstein, Moishe Goodman, Abraham Rovner and Shloime Zietz.

United Garment Workers Union, Local 83

It was in the period leading up to 1912, the years of which Dr. J. L. Hamil, Mr. David Stein of the Amalgamated and Mr. Abraham Kirzner of the International spoke so nostalgically, that the first steps were taken by the men's tailors to organize a union of their own. At that time there were a number of people who had a good deal of influence with the workers — they were Mr. Sam Fasser, one of the leaders of the Socialist League; Mr. Isaac Matenko, a prominent Toronto teacher and one of the founders of the United Garment Workers Union, Local 83; Mr. Salutsky, head of the local Bund organization; the brothers Rosenfeld; Mr. Savitzky; and the poet Mr. Aron Glantz-Leyeles, today an important figure in American Jewish journalism.

Some of those closely associated with the founding of the men's tailors union were Mr. S. M. Shapiro, its first secretary — now the publisher and editor of the Toronto *Hebrew Journal*; Mr. Joseph Stein, formerly chairman of the local; Mr. Rosenbloom, manager of the United Workers Union and later chairman of the Amalgamated; Mr. Maidonick; Mr. Tovey, a Gentile; Mr. Markowitz; and Mr. Sol Spivak, president of the Amalgamated for the past fifteen years.

The new union Local 83 was a failure from the start. The majority of the workers in the men's wear industry consisted of former yeshiva students and former socialists, none of whom were then ready for the idea of trade unionism. Many were holding down their first jobs at the T. Eaton Company clothing factory where the average wage was about $6 a week. Some worked for the Lowndes Company, one of the oldest Gentile shops in the city. A few joined the new union but their enthusiasm was usually short-lived. One week the union functioned; the next, so to say, it was out of existence. However, the union somehow did manage to struggle along until the time of the T. Eaton strike. With the smashing of this strike, Local 83 folded up for good.

Among the more active union members a bitterness developed towards the international headquarters of the United Garment Workers Union, of which Local 83 was a branch. They felt betrayed by the parent home organization which had not given them any help whatever during the strike. We cannot deal here with all the strikes in which Jewish workers took part in those years — the general strikes, for instance, or the work stoppages in individual shops. But one strike of unusual interest is the one that took place in the Randall and Johnston Company. According to Mr. David Stein the strike was a response by the Jewish workers to the discriminatory policy of the firm, which forbade a Jewish girl working in the factory to have her meals in the employee lunch room. The strike was a violent one and lasted an entire summer and in the end the union lost out.

Thus it is apparent that the first unions had a very tough time of it. There were frequent embittered conflicts between the shops and the unions. But although the unions suffered one defeat after another, there crystallized nevertheless in the minds of the workers a belief that victory would eventually be theirs.

During the first decade of the century the United Garment Workers Union, an American Federation of Labor (AFL) organization, was well established in the men's clothing industry both in the United States and Canada. The national officers, though men of integrity, had little understanding of the temperament of Jewish immigrant workers. The conduct of the national officers of the United Garment Workers in their negotiations with the employers in a series of major strikes from Chicago to New York created a feeling of distrust among the clothing workers. Relations between the national office and the New York locals of Jewish tailors became severely strained after union officials accepted a compromise offer to end a 1912 general strike involving more than 11,000 clothing workers. The settlement, secretly arrived at, was denounced by the strike leaders and poisoned relations between the Jewish tailors and the United Garment Workers Union.

At a convention in Nashville, Tennessee, more than 100 delegates, representing an unquestioned majority of the New York membership, were refused seats. In anger the opposition members left the hall, convened at another hotel, and declared themselves the legally constituted convention of the United Garment Workers. In 1914 the dissident members formed the Amalgamated Clothing Workers of America which within a few years consolidated its hold on the clothing industry, the United Garment Workers being reduced to a subsidiary branch. The Amalgamated was for a time a member of the AFL, then became a pillar of strength in the Congress of Industrial Organizations. The Toronto delegates to the historic convention in Nashville were Mr. I. Lesser, Mr. Joseph Stein, Mr. Yaffe and Mr. Kleinman. The Toronto delegates fully endorsed the new union, and as a result Local 83 of the United Garment Workers was dissolved and replaced by a local of the Amalgamated.

The Amalgamated Union and Its Accomplishments

In 1915, one year after the Amalgamated was founded, Mr. Sidney Hillman, its president, was invited to Toronto by the local union. He conducted negotiations with the local manufacturers and succeeded in winning for the workers union recognition, the forty-four hour week, and time and a half for overtime. It was the first collective bargaining agreement to be signed in Canada. A board of arbitration, with Professor McMillan of the

University of Toronto as first chairman, was formed in 1915 and here again the credit belongs to Mr. Hillman.

From 1916 to 1930 the Amalgamated union strongly consolidated its position in the men's clothing industry. With the exception of a bitter factional dispute that flared up with certain leftist elements in the union, the reign of the Amalgamated has to date been marked by peace and quiet. Its influence in labour ranks is enormous and it has won the respect of the entire community. The honour paid to Mr. Sol Spivak, the union's manager, who was elected first vice-president of the powerful Canadian Congress of Labour, is a token of the esteem in which the union is held in Canadian labour circles.

The Amalgamated Clothing Workers Union has a membership of 3,500 today of whom half are Jewish. The Amalgamated has been instrumental in bringing to Canada a large number of Jewish tailors from the displaced persons camps of Europe. It has always been prominent in philanthropic activities, its members frequently assessing themselves a day's pay for the Histadrut and other causes, Gentile as well as Jewish.

By a recent decision of the neutral chairman, Professor Jacob Finkelman, the 3,500 members of the Toronto Joint Board were awarded retirement pensions to be paid for by the clothing industry. The fund is to be administered by a board of trustees with equal representation from the union and the employers. The employers began contributing 3% of their payrolls for this plan on April 1, 1950. In his decision, Professor Finkelman pointed out that the clothing industry has stood in the forefront of new advances in industrial relations. The Amalgamated is thus the first labour union in Canada to obtain an industry-paid pension fund, and it is expected that it will set the pattern for other industries in the Dominion. Mr. Sol Spivak, manager of the Toronto Joint Board, led the movement for retirement pensions.

The Toronto Joint Board, under Mr. Spivak's management, was the first labour union in the Dominion of Canada to extract the concession of paid holidays and paid vacations, and the first to establish a welfare program maintained by employers' payroll contributions. The length of its harmonious relations with the employers is also a record in the industrial life of Canada. It is noteworthy that in only a few major cases was it necessary to submit matters to arbitration. As a rule problems were solved and settlements arrived at through direct negotiations.

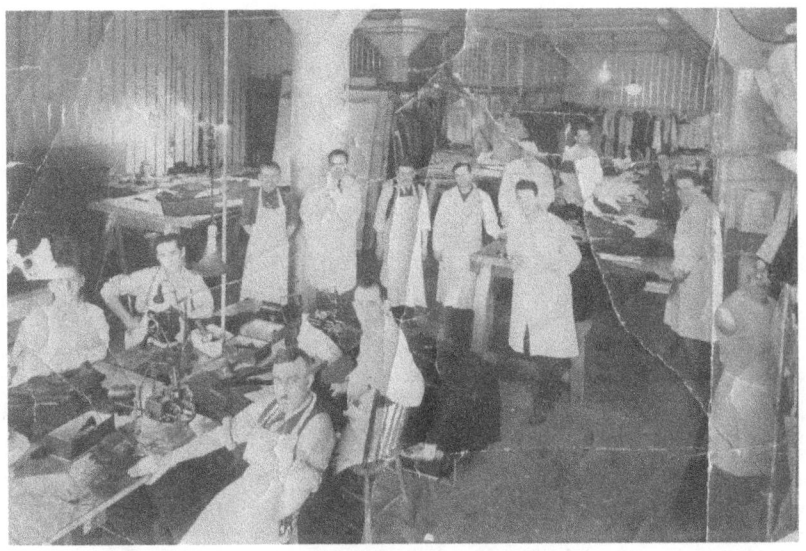

Interior of Toronto Fur Shop
Undated photograph, possibly from the 1920s or earlier. Although few in number, Jewish fur workers formed their own union in which meetings were usually conducted in Yiddish.

The joint board here has not only brought complete unionization to the Toronto market but under Mr. Spivak's direction has helped to organize and bring under collective bargaining agreements clothing, shirt, cotton garment and glove factories throughout Ontario. The joint board is also a very influential factor in the political life of the province and the Dominion. Indeed it can be truthfully said that the Amalgamated Clothing Workers Union has always taken a foremost part in defending the interest of Canadian workers, Gentile as well as Jewish, and that it has always been ready, morally and financially, to stand behind every worthy cause.

⤳ The Fur Trade

The fur manufacturing industry is unique among the needle trades. It is a specialized field in which mass production methods have not taken root and in which most of the work is still done by hand. In the early 1900s there were no manufacturers as we know them today, most furs being sold by merchants who had their own workshops and sold directly to the public. Some of the first Jews to open their own establishments in Toronto were Mr. Charles Draimin, Mr. Louis Freifeld, Mr. M. Hartman and Mr.

Labour Day Parade, Early 1900s, Showing Brodey–Draimin Furs
Brodey–Draimin Furs is shown at its Yonge Street location. Partners Isaac Brodey and Charles
Draimin, his brother-in-law, were presidents of Goel Tzedec and Holy Blossom respectively.

Joseph Schwartz. Most of the leading fur manufacturers today such as Frank and Joe Schipper of Schipper Freifeld Company, Max Menkes, Jack Bender and Harry Englander, of A. Englander and Son, learned the fur trade in these early Jewish factories.

Although Jewish fur manufacturers entered the picture as early as 1910, it is significant that as late as 1920 there were only three large Jewish firms, namely Brodey and Draimin, the J. P. Schwartz Fur Company and the Graner Robin Fur Company. The Furriers Protective Association, an organization formed by the fur manufacturers, consisted chiefly of Gentile businessmen. The Jewish fur manufacturers, unlike those in the other needle trades, came largely from outside the industry. Few joined the Furriers Protective Association, instead founding an organization of their own, the Independent Fur Manufacturers Association.

The number of Jewish workers engaged in fur was very small and as late as 1920 there were no Jewish members in the two fur unions, for male and female workers respectively. With the stream of Jewish immigration flowing into Canada after the First World War the picture rapidly changed. Jews increasingly began to enter the fur trade in Montreal and Winnipeg as well as Toronto. By 1923 there came into existence an exclusively Yiddish fur local in Toronto, Local 40, where meetings at first were conducted entirely in Yiddish. The new immigrants had not yet learned to speak English and felt uncomfortable about joining the two English locals in the city.

In 1923 a general strike was called by the leaders of Local 40 in an effort to organize the entire fur trade. Mr. Kaufman, president of the International Fur Union, arrived in Toronto to lend his assistance. After four weeks the strike was settled, the manufacturers yielding to all the strikers' demands. By 1923 the workers had gained recognition for their union, shorter hours and higher wages. At that time there were eighteen Jewish-owned shops in the city and all recognized the union. Unfortunately friction developed between the union officers and the rank and file of the membership. A Communist-led group tried to discredit and overthrow the union leadership, which was ideologically inclined towards the leftist Poalei Zion.

The struggle for control lasted for seven years, with the Gentile unions supporting the officers of the local. Some of the more prominent leaders of the Poalei Zion faction were Mr. Max Federman, Mr. N. Simon, Mr. Berel Maimon, Mr. I. Zisapel and Mr. Kirshenbaum. In the end the leadership of Local 40 succeeded in suppressing the dissidents and they have since been in control of the union. This local struggle was a prelude to the greater struggle that convulsed the Furriers International Union in which Ben Gold, president of the national office and Max Federman, manager of the local branch, figured so prominently.

The manufacturing of fur collars and cuffs sprang up in the late 1920s as a specialized junior branch of the fur industry. The Collar and Cuffs Manufacturers Association, an organization for employers in the trade, and Local 100, a union for fur workers, appeared on the industrial scene at about the same time. From the first the majority of the workers in collars and cuffs, and most of the manufacturers were Jewish. Pioneers in this branch were Mr. Joseph Levine, Mr. Israel Winebar, Mr. Joseph Kerbel, Mr. Benny Ross and Mr. Dorfman.

During the late 1920s there were about thirty-five collar and cuff shops in the city and in the space of a short time the industry became firmly established among the needle trades. Shortly after the Communist-influenced dissidents failed in their attempt to capture control of the union, a second general strike was called. This time, after only a week, the unions won a quick settlement and emerged greatly strengthened, with all their demands granted.

For a time the industry was calm. Then, like a bolt from the blue, a

Brodey-Draimin's
October Presentation of
FINE FURS

All summer long our factory has been busy evolving new fashions for the Fall and Winter season. Here is what we did. We took furs bought early in the Spring when prices were at the lowest and made them into the season's newest and smartest models. This gives you a choice of furs at the lowest price of 1933 made into the smartest fashions of 1934. We urge you to come and see the new coats. We know you will be delighted with the styles and wonderful values.

BUY WITH CONFIDENCE
—Furs Restyled at Moderate Prices—

Brodey-Draimin
Fur Company

256 Yonge St.   AD. 1087
Branches—Hamilton and Kitchener

Ads for Brodey–Draimin Furs, 1933, and Herman Furs, 1924

The finest type of Fur Garments procurable —Coats that show their worth in the excellence of workmanship, the luxurious linings and the becoming styles.

HUDSON SEAL	PERSIAN LAMB
RACCOON	MUSKRAT
ELECTRIC SEAL	MOLESKIN

Every fur coat and piece is made in our factory by skilled workers and absolutely guaranteed.

Direct From Our Factory at a Saving of 35% to 50%

E. Herman Co., Limited
61 Gerrard St. West—College and Bay Cars to the Door
Open Daily Till 8.30 p.m.—Special Attention to Mail Orders.

fresh conflict erupted between the two Gentile unions and the two Jewish locals. There were strong differences of opinion over the way local union affairs were being managed. Eventually the disputing parties turned over their differences to the District Trades and Labour Council for arbitration. A joint board for all the fur unions was created and a neutral conciliation officer appointed by the council. At that time Mr. Max Federman headed Local 40 and Mr. Harry Simon Local 100. We cannot here write the full story of the furriers' unions but one thing is plain — the fur unions were seldom free from one sort of crisis or another.

The fur trade, a luxury trade of course, was especially hard hit by the Depression of the 1930s. Many firms had to shut down and many workers were thrown out of work. Fearing the effect that cheap labour in other fur centres might have on the industry in general, the local unions sent agents to Montreal and to Winnipeg to help organize the fur workers there. Mr. Federman speaks ironically today of the frequent weekend "excursions" (the railway fare was substantially reduced for weekend trips) that his union authorized him to make for organizing purposes. To Winnipeg went Mr. Harry Simon to organize the fur workers there. Both met with considerable success and in a short time the first all-Canadian conference was called to lay the foundations for one strong union for the whole fur trade.

Today almost 75% of the fur workers and most of the manufacturers in Toronto are Jewish. In Montreal most of the manufacturers but only 25% of the workers are Jewish. In Winnipeg only 30% of the workers are Jewish but the manufacturers, in the main, are still Jewish. There are now fifty-three union shops in Toronto with an active union membership of 500. The unions have become strong and respected. The workers have acquired union recognition, an agreement for a forty-hour week, a vacation clause providing two weeks paid vacation after one year of employment, a welfare fund covering sickness and hospitalization, and an insurance scheme giving the beneficiary of every worker $75 in the event of death. In other cities, particularly Montreal and Winnipeg, the situation has vastly improved, with the workers receiving the same benefits as here.

Despite the internal conflicts that almost destroyed the union, despite the violent and bitter feuds between the different factions fighting for control (a story that cannot be dealt with here in detail), the union survived and prospered, becoming firmly entrenched in the industry, and winning wide recognition in Canadian labour circles.

The Leather and Pocket Book Industry

There are several other industries in which Jews have gained important footholds. In the baking trade, for instance, Jewish workers now have a strong union; the employers too are organized as the Association of Jewish Bakers. An increasing number of Jews are now going into the manufacturing of jewellery and costume jewellery, and a considerable number are working at these trades. Jews are well represented in the footwear industry, both in the manufacturing and selling ends. However, the foregoing industries do not come under the head of needle trades. Among the needle trades that we have not yet dealt with is the leather goods industry.

The leather and pocket book industry ranks fourth among the needle trades in the number of Jewish workers involved and in the proportion of Jews among the manufacturers. There are twelve of these Jewish manufacturers in Toronto today and several of the longest established are the National Leather Goods, with Mr. Dave Wilson as president; Progressive Leather Goods with Mr. Harry Rumm as president; and Paragon Leather Goods, with Mr. Albert Mandel as president. Most of the other shops are owned by former needle workers, men who made their way up from the work bench. The leather workers' union was organized by Mr. Glass and has a membership of 300. In spite of his heavy duties as head of the union Mr. Glass has found time to take an active part in the affairs of the local Jewish community. Asked for information about the growth of his union, Mr. Glass furnished us with the following outline.

The International Handbag Workers Union was organized in 1930 at the start of the Depression. Workers in the handbag trade were hard hit; employment was hard to find and wages were pitifully low. When an experienced operator did get a job he was lucky if he found $15 in his pay envelope at the end of the week. The hardships that the workers were going through did not keep the employers from trying to lower wages still more, nor from increasing the number of working hours from forty-four to forty-nine.

If a worker dared to protest, he was summarily dismissed. Fired from one shop, he would be barred from the others, the employers uniting in an unspoken agreement to keep out potential malcontents. Realizing that without an organization to defend their interest their jobs would remain insecure and working conditions bad, the workers at long last banded together and formed a union.

It was in 1932 that a small group of workers assembled in the Radomer Hall at 210 Beverley Street and at the conclusion of an enthusiastic meeting, founded the Pocket Workers Union. Without losing any time the leaders proceeded to map out a campaign for organizing the workers in the trade. Special tact was necessary, for many of the workers were Gentile and most of the Jewish workers were Yiddish-speaking immigrants unfamiliar with the English tongue. The task was not an easy one and the workers had to undergo a lengthy period of indoctrination before they were ready to be unionized. In the end all the obstacles were surmounted and the trade organized with most of the workers joining up. Through their union the workers then demanded union recognition, higher pay and the forty-four-hour week.

The demands for wage boosts were rejected outright and the union retaliated by calling a general strike. All shops, union and non-union, organized and unorganized, responded promptly. The work stoppage was complete; the trade was paralyzed. Nevertheless the strike came to an abrupt end, failing completely after only a few days, and with its collapse the union folded. All that had been so slowly and painfully built up was wiped out in a day. The failure of the strike brought serious consequences in its train; the employers became more harsh and peremptory, working conditions got worse, and known unionists were fired from their jobs, many of them being compelled to leave the city after fruitlessly seeking other employment.

What brought about the collapse of the strike? We cannot go into all the reasons but one of the chief causes was the debut of the Congress of Industrial Organizations on the Canadian labour scene. The new CIO movement advocated a single union for an entire industry rather than separate unions for each craft or branch on an industry. The rivalry between the new industrial unions and long-established craft unions split the ranks of labour wide open. Some joined the new organization; others fought it, charging that the CIO leaders adhered too closely to the communist party line. As the young leather workers' union was not affiliated with any international union, leftist elements gained control of it and handed it over to the CIO camp. This action sealed the fate of the strike. Many workers, especially the Gentile ones, withdrew from the union, refusing to be associated with an organization they regarded as communistic. Upon their return to work the strike ended and the union broke up.

Three years passed before a new leather workers' union was organized in 1935. Its leaders remembered well the lessons of 1932 and took special precautions against repeating the former errors. A powerful leather workers organization had grown up in New York with strong locals in Chicago, Philadelphia and other American cities. Contact was established with headquarters of the International in New York and its president, Mr. Isadore Lederman, came here to help organize the Toronto local. Work was carried on clandestinely until there were enough members and then, in 1936, new union demands were submitted to the employers.

These called for union recognition, increased pay, a forty-four-hour week, and time and a half for overtime. Direct negotiations proved ineffectual and a general strike was called. Despite a lukewarm response on the part of some shops, particularly those involving Gentile workers, the walkout was a success. Recognized labour leaders of other unions, such as Mr. Max Federman (who actually led the strike), Mr. Harry Simon, organizer for the American Federation of Labour, and Mr. David Stein, business agent for the Amalgamated, threw their support behind the strikers. Many local unions and other progressive organizations furnished moral and financial support. The headquarters of the International Union sent down Mr. Sam Lederman, head of the strong Chicago local.

The struggle, sharp and bitter, lasted for four weeks and in the end the union, chiefly because of the help it received from other organizations, was victorious. While all of its demands were not met, the union won recognition for itself, and time and a half for overtime. The union was pleased with the terms, believing that a good start was made with recognition of the union as a bargaining agent. The leather workers' union is now a member of the Canadian Congress of Labour and is affiliated with the AFL.

Although relatively small in membership, the union supports all worthy causes in the Jewish community. Last year each individual worker donated twelve hours for the Histadrut campaign; a total of $1,500 was collected. The present officers of the Toronto local are Mr. Ted Schwimmer, president; Mr. L. Warshawsky, vice-president; Mr. Marvin Lister, secretary-treasurer; Mr. S. Katz, recording secretary; and Mr. Moishe Glass, business agent. Other active members of the local executive are Mr. Eddie Bidle, Mr. A. Glass, Miss Vera Poller, Miss Mary Denison, Mr. L. Rosenburg, Mr. Sam Kolinum, Mr. Gordon Leach and Mr. Bill Brown.

"Yiddish flows in torrents."

Afterword:
Recollections and Experiences of the Jewish Press in Toronto
By Ben Kayfetz

MY REMARKS ON THE JEWISH PRESS in Toronto must not be mistaken for any kind of definitive study. They are only my highly subjective, very personal, very imperfectly recalled observations based on my exposure to the Jewish periodicals of the city since childhood, going back some fifty-five years.

My first experience was with *Der Yiddisher Zhurnal*, which carried the English name the *Hebrew Journal* even though it was written in Yiddish, not in Hebrew. Possibly, back in 1913 when the paper was established, the feeling was still prevalent in certain circles that "Jewish" was too stark a word, and "Hebrew" more refined. It appeared six days a week, every day but Saturday, and met the needs of the immigrant population for five decades. In my own case, at *cheder* my Hebrew teacher spent a few minutes with me every day going over the *"Neies Bei Unz in Shtot"* section of the paper, which was a summation of the local general news — a story involving a Jewish peddler who was arrested, a theft here, a violent robbery or hold-up there — all culled from the metropolitan downtown press. This daily review gave me a personal intimacy with the Yiddish press, which has never left me to this day.

Throughout its history the *Zhurnal* had to withstand stiff

competition from the three (and earlier four) Yiddish New York dailies, which were on sale in Toronto on the same day they were published. There was a joke that circulated in the city — it was similarly told in New York about the *Tog* and *Forverts* — "How did the *Toronto Star* find out a full day in advance what news reports the *Zhurnal* would publish the next day?" In New York, it was the *Times* in place of the *Star*, but the implication of "scissors and paste" and quick translation was the same.

It is probable that when the *Forverts, Morgen Zhurnal, Tageblatt* and *Tog*, all of New York, were publishing, their combined circulation in Toronto was far greater than that of the *Zhurnal*. This sort of competition is something the *Globe*, the *Telegram* and the *Star* never had to endure. Yet the amazing thing is that the *Zhurnal* survived as long as it did into the 1960s. It lasted twenty years longer than similar Yiddish dailies in American cities with much larger Jewish populations — Chicago, Cincinnati, Boston, Philadelphia and Cleveland — whose daily, local Yiddish papers expired in the early 1940s. For the most part, in the 1950s there were no Yiddish dailies anywhere in the United States outside of New York City; while in Canada, the *Kanader Adler* in Montreal and *Zhurnal* in Toronto were still appearing six days a week.

The editor, Shmuel (Samuel) M. Shapiro, had a group of "angels" he would turn to when the paper needed an infusion of money, or when the creditors were getting impatient. Among the backers were Ben Sadowski of Toronto, Sam Bronfman of Montreal, and Melech Grafstein of London, Ontario, who was the landlord of the paper's premises at 542 Dundas Street West in Toronto. But Grafstein withdrew his patronage in a dispute about editorial control. Within a few months Shapiro and the paper moved to new quarters at College and Lippincott Avenue where the paper remained for approximately ten years.

The exchanges in the *Zhurnal* were often fierce, and many talented writers contributed. Both editorial views and styles were highly personal. For example, when Shapiro, under a pseudonym, referred to one of his backers and contributing writers as a "graphoman," their collaboration ended for good. In the world of Yiddish writing, there is nothing more offensive than being called a graphoman. It is a bit of a surprise that this useful expression of Greek origin has not entered the English language. A graphoman is someone who suffers from the disease of graphomania, an extreme obsession with writing without the commensurate and required talent that should accompany it.

It is difficult now and in English to evoke the personal and ideological fire of Canada's Yiddish-language journalism. Perhaps one experience of my own out of the recent past can recapture the flavour. In 1956 — I was then on the staff of the Canadian Jewish Congress — I had just returned from a trip to Winnipeg. Shortly afterwards an article appeared in *Vochenblatt*, the communist weekly, which included the ritual denunciations of Max Federman and other renegades from the working class. But this time the attack was different. The editor, Joshua Gershman, had found someone lower than Federman. In fact these were the exact words: "*S'iz do eyner vos er iz nideriker fun Federman!*" ["There is someone who is even lower than Federman!"] I read on impatiently to see who this unspeakable wretch could be, and there was the name in boldface, "*Un dos iz Ben Kayfetz!*" No matter what justification ideological enmities and certainties provided, personal attacks in the Yiddish press left people with many scars and long memories.

The *Zhurnal*, I must admit, never had the prestige that its Montreal counterpart, the *Adler (Eagle)*, enjoyed. It never pretended to be anything more than it was — a provincial daily serving the needs and interests of a very local public. Shapiro gathered around him a number of talented and able writers. There was Moishe Fogel, who had a daily column in the paper; Itzchok Feigelman, who wrote European-style "feuilletons"; and Nachman Shemen, who wrote under his own name and various pen-names. Most of these writers were also Hebrew teachers as well, or had been teachers previously. Gershon Pomerantz undertook the editorship of *Der Yiddisher Zhurnal* in its last two years as a regular daily newspaper. He thoroughly enjoyed this position: denouncing and criticising right and left, reprinting his literary criticism, poems and reviews and putting out the entire paper himself, typesetting the editorials right into hot type. But eventually ill-health forced him to give up the paper.

In 1935 because of an editorial dispute at the *Zhurnal*, a new Yiddish publication was created, the weekly *Kanader Neies (Canadian News)*, which was published and edited by Morris Goldstick and his sister Mrs. Dorothy Dworkin in Toronto. This was not sold across the counter, but was distributed as an insert with the weekend edition of the New York Yiddish papers of which Mrs. Dworkin was the distributing agent. The paper appealed to both major ideological elements in the Jewish community

— pro-Bundist, because Mrs. Dworkin continued the tradition of her late husband Henry Dworkin who was active in the socialist movement, and pro-Zionist, because Morris Goldstick was a devoted Zionist. The paper lasted twenty years, ending publication in 1955.

There was also a third Yiddish paper in Toronto that I recall. It was officially considered a New York paper, yet the advertising and much of the writing, editing and printing was done in Toronto. This was the *Proletarisher Gedank*, the organ of a very small minority group, the leftist Poalei Zion. The Jewish or rather Yiddish-speaking communist movement in Toronto had a long history of having their own press organ. Their first paper was called, appropriately, *Der Kampf* (*The Struggle*), and its first editor was Philip Halpern. In 1939 during the non-aggression pact between Nazi Germany and Soviet Russia, the Communist party was illegal. The newspaper's name was changed to *Der Veg* (The Road). And after the war when the party was respectable, at least for a few years, the name *Vochenblatt* (*Canadian Jewish Weekly*) was adopted. The long-time editor was Joshua Gershman, and when his health failed about two or three years ago, the paper stopped publishing. It was not, of course, self-sustaining. Gershman himself would take a Canada-wide trip once or twice a year to raise funds to keep the paper going. The contributors and co-editors included the cartoonist Avrom Yanofsky, Harry Guralnick, Joe Salsberg and Sholem Shtern of Montreal.

Before I leave the *Zhurnal*, let me say something about its English page, a feature it acquired in the late 1930s. Its first editor was the late Moses Frank, the former publisher-editor of the *Jewish Standard*. He also wrote a daily news commentary in the *Zhurnal*. The succeeding editor of the English page was David Rome, who served from January 1940 to November 1942. He was followed by Ben Lappin who held the position for one year. Leo Hayman, Rabbi H. Goodman and Nathan Cohen were also editors.

What was happening in the meantime in the English-language Jewish press? Not very much, I am constrained to say, at least not until 1930. The *Canadian Jewish Review* had been founded in Toronto in 1921 by George and Florence Freedlander Cohen from the United States. This was a publication that paid great attention to social notes — comings and goings to the Catskills, the Adirondacks and the Laurentians, detailed descriptions of what the bride wore, who held the baby boy at the *briss* and who poured tea at any given reception. Soon after Ontario introduced the government-supervised sale of liquor but, unlike Quebec, still did not permit its commercial advertising, the *Review* moved its main office (as did other periodicals) from Toronto to Montreal to take advantage of this advertising revenue. It now became a two-city weekly, establishing a precedent which has been followed today by the *Canadian Jewish News*.

The *Review* did not appear to pursue any structured editorial policy with regard to Jewish politics. What it did subscribe to was a mild non-Zionism, even extending sometimes to anti-Zionism, perhaps reflecting the middle class, culturally assimilated, older American and "classical reform" background of its founders. Non-Zionism was quite acceptable in those days. The American Jewish Committee, B'nai B'rith and most of the reformed rabbis were non-Zionist, including Rabbi Eisendrath who came to Holy Blossom Synagogue in 1929, and who contributed a weekly column to the *Review*.

The 1929 attack on the Jews at the Wailing Wall in Jerusalem and in Hebron put the entire Jewish world in turmoil. The Zionists, led by Mrs. Rose Dunkelman, were terribly frustrated. There was no place that the Zionist point of view could be put forward to reach the English-speaking Jews and the general non-Jewish Canadian public. So Mrs. Dunkelman started her own paper in 1930, the *Jewish Standard*.

In his two years as its editor, Meyer Weisgal made quite an impact on Toronto Jewish journalism. He continued his practice of inviting contributions from world-renowned writers, and in the next few years, the *Jewish Standard* ran original, commissioned articles by Dorothy Thompson, Pierre Van Paassen and Winston Churchill. Weisgal used his Zionist Organization of America contacts to get writers like Louis Lipsky, Felix Frankfurter, Nahum Sokolow and Menachem Ussishkin. In this way Weisgal turned the *Jewish Standard* into an international journal, which happened to be published in Toronto. But the Depression of the 1930s and his free hand with money were incompatible factors. Eventually Weisgal left Toronto to do other things, after which the *Standard* went steadily downhill. The ownership went through many vicissitudes and changeovers from 1932 to 1937. It was sold to non-Jewish publishing firms — J. Laird Thompson, the Age Publishing Company on Willcocks Street and, for a while, it was one of the Maclean–Hunter stable of periodicals. It then fell into the hands of Moses Z. Frank whom we mentioned earlier. Frank was a good editor, but not as good a businessman. In 1937 Julius Hayman, then thirty years old, a newcomer from Winnipeg who had been the paper's former business manager and had started a rival periodical, the *Jewish Sentinel*, bought the *Standard* from Frank for under $1,000 and finally brought stability to the publication as its editor-publisher.

There was a long period through the 1940s and 1950s when Toronto had no English-language Jewish weekly. The *Jewish Standard* was at various times a monthly and a fortnightly, but never a weekly, and the *Review* had moved to Montreal. It was not until 1960 that M. J. Nurenberger switched languages and the *Canadian Jewish News* appeared as a weekly in English.

Archie Bennett was probably the first bilingual Jewish journalist in Canada. He used to contribute to the *Kanader Adler* and was the first truly national journalist we had in eastern Canada. Being raised in Kingston, he was open to both Toronto and Montreal. He wrote for the old *Jewish Times* of Montreal, the *Jewish Chronicle* of Montreal, the *Canadian Jewish Review* when it was in Toronto and Montreal and, in the last twenty-five years or so, for the *Jewish Standard* in Toronto. As a young man in the summer break from teaching at Queen's University in Kingston, he was editor of the *Canadian Jewish Times* in Montreal. There were various other personalities marginally linked with the Toronto Jewish press in the past. Cantor Nathan Stolnitz and Israel Plattner both contributed to the *Zhurnal*. Another contributor to the Toronto Yiddish press was a streetcar conductor, S. Nepom, whom I knew from my days as a newsboy on the corner of Roncesvalles Avenue and Queen Street, and who wrote for the *Adler*, the *Zhurnal* and the leftist *Kampf*.

Despite the rhetoric of the Yiddishists, the Yiddish press in Canada is receding into the past and the English-language Jewish press has become more of an impersonal nationwide operation. I am rather pleased, looking back at it, that I was around in the era when journalism was still a business for individuals. Do not misunderstand what I am saying. I am not looking back nostalgically to a better day. The public, I am sure, is better served today. But while it lasted, it was enjoyable, and I am delighted that I can recall such episodes. [*1984*] ⇾

⇾ *Toronto-born Benjamin G. Kayfetz (1916–2002) was a long-time director of public relations for Canadian Jewish Congress. He campaigned tirelessly to protect minority rights and wrote many articles for Jewish and mainstream publications. The above essay was previously published in the Summer 1984 issue of Polyphony, the journal of the Multicultural Historical Society of Ontario.*

Rodamer Friendly Society, Third Jubilee Banquet, 1928
Landsmanschaft organizations such as the Rodamer Friendly Society, consisting largely of immigrant families from the same town or geographic region, were numerous in Toronto of the 1920s.

Glossary

anshei. Hebrew word meaning "men of" or "people of," as in *Anshei Minsk*, people of Minsk. Many landsmanschaft synagogues were named by this formula.

Bundist. Adherent of a Jewish socialist and secular movement founded in the Russian Empire in 1897 and violently suppressed there after 1917, while gaining many followers in Europe and America.

baal tefillah (Hebrew) Leader of prayer services for a minyan or congregation.

challah, traditional braided bread eaten on the Jewish Sabbath.

chaver, chaverim (pl). from Hebrew, "comrade." *Chaverim* denotes a circle of comrades or like-minded people.

cheder, chederim (pl.) Literally a "room" (Hebrew); refers to an old-fashioned classroom where Jewish education could be obtained, often from a *melamed* (teacher) with a *Gemorah* (Talmudic tract) in one hand and ruler in the other.

chevra (Hebrew) A friendly circle or group, as in *Chevra Shas*, a group of students who meet regularly to study the Talmud.

Agudas Hamishpocha, 1937
The Agudas Hamishpocha (United Families Organization) was a landsmanschaft-type society founded in Toronto in 1928 for members of the extended Rubinoff, Naftolin & Arnoff families and friends.

farein, fareinin (pl.) (Yiddish) A society or societies, such as a sick benefit society or the Toronto Folksfarein, often dedicated to the betterment of its members.

genossen (Yiddish) beneficiaries; persons who stand to gain.

Hassidism (Hebrew) A popular religious movement in Judaism started by the Ba'al Shem Tov in the late 1700s, characterized by an emphasis on doing charitable deeds, the joy of obeying the commandments, and a messianic fervour. Adherents of the *Hassidic* movement are called *Hassidim*.

kashruth (Hebrew) The kosher status of foodstuffs, cooking utensils and the environment in which they are stored, handled and prepared, all of which are strictly regulated under Jewish law.

klausen, small home or "storefront" congregation; a *shtibl*.

landsmanschaft, landsmanschaften (pl) (Yiddish) Group or groups formed by immigrants coming from the same home town or from the same region. Usually a religious congregation or secular organization such as a mutual benefit society.

landsmen, landsleit (Yiddish) Persons from the same home town or close geographical region in the old country, and deriving a sense of kinship thereby.

Maskalah (Hebrew) Followers of the Haskalah or Enlightenment movement in Judaism that flourished in the 19th century and attempted to modernize many aspects of the ancient religious tradition and culture, and to admit modern scientific and secular knowledge into the Jewish world-view.

melamed, melamdim (pl) Old-fashioned Hebrew teacher of the European variety, always learned in the Holy Scriptures and exegetical texts although not always in modern educational methods.

mohel (Hebrew) Rabbi or other person trained to perform medical-religious ritual of circumcision.

Poalei Zion (Hebrew, "Workers of Zion") Jewish nationalistic socialist–labour movement that gained popularity in the early 20th century.

schoichet (Hebrew; also Yiddish) Ritual slaughterer of kosher meat.

sefer Torah (Hebrew) A book or scroll of the Torah.

shammus. Sexton of a synagogue.

shofar (Hebrew) Ram's-horn trumpet traditionally sounded at Rosh Hashana and Yom Kippur.

siddur (Hebrew, literally "order" as in the "order of prayers.") Jewish prayer-book.

s'micha, also *semicha* (Hebrew) Rabbinical ordination.

shtibl, also *shtübl* (Yiddish) Small home or "storefront" congregation.

Tsadik, tsadikim (pl.) (Hebrew) Person or persons of extraordinary piety, good deeds and religious devotion.

Yehudim (Hebrew) Name by which rich German-Jewish immigrants in North America were popularly known a century ago.

Photographs & Illustrations

Portrait, Shmuel Meyer Shapiro 9
Site of Toronto's First Minyan (Coomb's Drugstore) 11
Section of Downtown Toronto 12
Restaurant in the Ward 15
Newspaper Sketches of Peddlers in the Ward 18
Day of Atonement, 1910 22
Landmarks of the Early Community, ca 1912 26
Christian Missionary in the Ward, 1912 31
Scott Mission, Spadina Avenue, 1949 32
Letterhead of Toronto Jewish Kitchen, 1932 33
Mozirer Sick Benefit Society, Dance Poster 34
Teachers of the National Radical School, 1911 36
Pioneers of the Toronto Cloakmakers Union 38
Early Staff Photo, Hebrew Journal 39
Scene from the Ward 40
Cartoon from a New York Yiddish Weekly, 1910 42
A Yiddish Print Shop, 113 Elizabeth Street, ca 1911 44
Hebrew Journal, Staff & Partners, ca 1920s 51
Ads from the Hebrew Journal 54
Street Scene in Toronto's "Jewish Quarter," 1912 55
Mastheads of Five Yiddish Publications 56
Rotenberg & Sons (Steamship Agents), 1913 62
Ward Classroom & Elizabeth Street Playground 64
Poster for Labor League Concert, Massey Hall, 1936 66
Pioneers of Beth Hamidrash HaGadol Chevra Tehillim 67
Nordheimer Pianos, King Street, 1846 68
Richmond Street Synagogue (Holy Blossom), 1875 to 1897 70
Holy Blossom on Bond Street, 1897 to 1937 73
Holy Blossom Temple, with Construction Photograph 75
Holy Blossom Temple, Drawing of Sanctuary 76
Rabbi Weinreb with Benjamin Kurtz, a Shoichet 80
Orthodox Rabbis Participate in March, Toronto, ca 1915 81
Machzikei Hadat Letterhead 83

Goel Tzedec — University Avenue Synagogue — 1924 84
Rare Photograph of Former Elm Street Synagogue, ca 1908 86
View of McCaul Street Synagogue, ca 1920s (& as Church in 1890s) 88
Rabbi Jacob Gordon, Rare Early Photograph 89
Ostrovtzer Shul Youth Orchestra, ca 1930 93
Ostrovtzer Shul, Cecil & Spadina, ca 1950 94
Rabbi Abraham Price 95
Kiever Synagogue 95
Rabbi Yudel Y. Rosenberg 97
Hassidic Wedding on Steps of Henry Street Synagogue, 1928 98
Henry Street Synagogue, by Aba Bayefsky 98
Leaflet Publicizing Husiatener Klaus Celebration, 1926 100
B'nai Israel — the Shaw Street Shul, Sanctuary & Exterior 102
Shaarei Shomayim on St. Clair Avenue 105
Opening of Shaarei Shomayim in Globe & Mail 106
Beth Sholom Synagogue 109
Rabbi David Monson with British Chief Rabbi Hertz 109
Tip Top Tailors, Newspaper Ad, 1920 110
ILGWU Workers on Strike, Toronto 1912 111
Joint Board Cloak, Skirt & Dressmakers Union, Toronto ca 1918 116
Summer Dresses & Fall Hats from M. Pullan & Sons, ca 1910 122
Anti-fascist Rally on Spadina Avenue, July 1933 124
Old-fashioned Sweatshop 129
Stereopticon View of Men's Cutting Room, T. Eaton Co., 1910 131
T. Eaton Company Store, Queen & Yonge Streets, 1920, & Ads 132
T. Eaton Company, View of Factory, 1921 133
Interior of Toronto Fur Shop 139
Labour Day Parade, Early 1900s, Showing Brodey-Draimin Furs 140
Ads for Brodey-Draimin Furs & E. Herman Fur Company 142
"Yiddish Flows in Torrents", Sketch ca 1910 147
Rodamer Friendly Society, Third Jubilee Banquet, 1928 153
Agudas Hamishpocha, 1937 154
Sample Page from Shapiro's Manuscript 158
View of Toronto from Waterfront, 1927 161

For many years, the religious head of the synagogue was the late Rabbi Jacob Gordon, who was born in Russia in 1877 and who dies in Toronto on 25th November, 1934. Originally Rabbi Gordon came to Toronto in the interests of the Wholoziner Yeshiva where he had been a student. He likes the city, and stayed on as head of the Beth Hamidrash Hagadol Chevra Tehilim. Rabbi Gordon was a scholar and author or outstanding merit, a man of wide secular as well as Talmudic knowledge. Friendly and approachable, he exercised a deep influence on the Toronto of his day and on the rest of the provinces as well. Rabbi Gordon helped to organise the Simcoe Street Talmud Torah and later its successor, t e Brunswick Ave. Talmud Torah. He personally taught in the latter school, and he was the man who introduced the study of oral Hebrew - Ivrith B'Ivrith into its classes.

In 1919, Rabbi Gordon was one of those instrumental in organising the Canadian Jewish Congress. Later he was one of the founders of the Mizrachi. He was active in many social and welfare activities and after the first world war he helped to bring into Canada many orphaned children. A fervent Zionist and staunchly orthodox, he naturally opposed the Reform movement - and the Rabbies who preached sermons on Christianity. He also battled the radical elements in the community - those who openly flouted the teaching of orthodoxy.

Besides being rabbi of the McCaull Street Synagogue, Rabbi Gordon was also rabbi of the Goel Tzedec, Shearith Israel, Tzemech Tzedek, and the Kenesseth Israel congregations. Since Rabbi Gordon's death, and particularly since Rabbi Reuben Slonim, a graduate of the Jewish Theological Seminary of New York (the Schechter Seminary) became its rabbi, the congregation has become conservative rather than orthodox - in the senses distinguished above. The McCaul Street Synagogue has more than 500 members now. The President of the Congregation is Mr. M. Kaufman.

THE RISE OF THE ANSHI CONGREGATIONS

Like many other Jewish communities in the new world the organised Toronto Jewish community emerged out of the small landsleit organisations that sprang up in the city with each new incoming wave of immigrants. The familiar Yiddish greeting "where does a Jew hail from" is often heard, even today, when old immigrants meet and a nostalgic longing for the old country is momentarily kindled by these encounters, which never fail

Sample page from Shapiro's manuscript.

A Note on the Text

The manuscript upon which this book is based is the property of Beth Tzedec Congregation. We are grateful to Ralph Berrin, a volunteer in the Beth Tzedec Museum, for bringing it to our attention, and to curator Dorion Liebgott for kindly loaning it to us to make this project possible. The manuscript consists of 127 double-spaced, typewritten pages on aged tracing paper, stored in a black three-ring binder.

The text was minimally edited for clarity and to correct errors of fact and spelling; some chapter and section heads were amended or added to better reflect the contents. In a few cases — such as in regards to the strike at the T. Eaton Company — the manuscript deals definitively with the same subject matter in more than one place; such material was consolidated and presented in the most logical spot. The chapter on "Synagogues, Congregations & Rabbis" was brought forward in the book as it was considered to be of greater interest to the general reader than the chapter on "Jews in the Needle Trade."

A few references in the manuscript to missing or unwritten sections suggest that its author intended a work of greater length, breadth and evenness. This may explain why "The Rise of the Toronto Jewish Community" (his own title for the work) was not published in his lifetime, although parts of it may have appeared originally in Yiddish as articles in the Daily Hebrew Journal.

All evidence indicates that the work was written in the late 1940s, with the latest amendments made in 1950. Its publication in 2010 makes this overlooked portrait of Toronto's early Jewish community — in many ways unsurpassed in colour and detail — accessible for the first time to the general reader and historian alike after sixty years of neglect.

Photo Credits

Front cover: Spadina Avenue, April 1957, photo by Walter Curtin, courtesy Library and Archives Canada e010745352 • Back cover: Goel Tzedec Synagogue 1928, courtesy Beth Tzedec Archives; interior of unidentified synagogue in Spadina area, April 1957, photo by Walter Curtin, courtesy Library and Archives Canada e010745348 • Page 15: City of Toronto Archives (CTA) s372-ss55-it51 • Page 22: Ontario Jewish Archives, photo 6719 • Page 30: CTA f1244-it2348 • Page 32: Photo by Gilbert Milne, Archives of Ontario (AO) C 3-1-0-0-514 • Page 44 (*bottom*): CTA s0372-ss0033-it0161 • Page 62: AO, I0021944 • Page 64 (*bottom*): CTA f200-s372-ss52-it72 • Page 84: AO, I0001320 (*top*); Beth Tzedec Archives (*bottom*) • Page 88 (*bottom*): CTA f1257-s1057-it990 • Page 98: Drawing by Aba Bayefsky, 1959, courtesy Evelyn Bayefsky • Page 109: Courtesy Beth Sholom Congregation • Page 111: Kheel Center for Labor, Cornell University, 5780P N45 F1600 • Page 116: Kheel Center for Labor, Cornell University, 5780P B3 F13A • Page 122 (*bottom*): CTA f1244-it0496 • Page 131: AO F-229-308-0-372, used with permission of Sears Canada Inc. • Page 133: AO, F 229-1-0-21 • Page 140: CTA f1568-it0314 • Thanks also to Holy Blossom, Beth Sholom, David Charles, Frances Ittleman, Sarah Kelman, Temi Rosenthal and Stella Barsh Rudolph, for generously providing other photographs used in this book.

View of Toronto from waterfront, with City Hall tower at left & St. James's steeple at right, 1927.

Index

Note: An asterisk (*) indicates a photograph or illustration.

- A -

Abend Zeitung, 40
Abramov, 24
Abramovitz, Z., 53
Abrams, A., 53
Abramsky, 13
Ackerman, Mendel, 53
Acme Cloak Co., 127-8
Adath Israel, 92
Aetna Cloaks, 127
Agudath Israel Anshei Sefarad (Palmerston Ave.) 104
Akiba, E., 54
Aleichem, Sholom, 35
Allen, 13
Almi, A., 53
Altman, J., 92
Amalgamated Clothing Workers of America, 137ff
American Federation of Labour, 137
Andrews, J., 105
"Anshei" congregations, rise of, 90
Anshei Apt, 91
Anshei Chmelnik, 91
Anshei Drildge, 91
Anshei Keltz, 91
Anshei Ostrovtze, 92
Anshei Shidlov, 91
Anshei Slipye, 92
Anshei Yivansk, 91
Anthony, Charles, 108
Apotov, David, 53
Arnoff, Moishe, 103
Associated Hebrew Free Schools, 104, 108
Association of Jewish Bakers, 144
Axler, Max, 89

- B -

Baal Shem Tov, 78
Babbit, Sender, 101
Babitch, M., 35
Bagot, Gov. Gen. Sir Charles, 69
bakery, first, 19
Barasch, Chaim, 87
Barondes, Joseph, 35
Bassin, Leib, Zisha & Motel, 95, 96
Baum, Berl, 53
Bay Street synagogue, 82
Bayefsky, Sam, 54
Beach Hebrew Institute (Beth Jacob) 104-5
Bender, Jack, 140
Benjamin brothers, 68
Benjamin, Frank, 130-31
Benjamin, L. M., 53
Bennett, 13
Bennett, Archie B., 47, 49
Berezovsky, Sam, 35
Berenstein, Lazar, 93
Berger, Mr. (shop chairman) 127
Berman, Max, 127
Bernstein, Cantor Akiva, 86
Beth Hamidrash HaGadol Chevra Tehillim, 67*, 86ff, 88*
Beth Jacob (Henry Street Synagogue), 96ff, 98*
Beth Sholom, 108ff, 109
Beth Yakov, see Beth Jacob
Beth Yehuda, 104
Biderman, Abraham, 95
Bidle, Eddie, 146
Blechman, Mr., 33
B'nei Israel (Shaw Street

161

shul) 101ff
B'nei Yakov, 105
Bond Street synagogue,
  see Holy Blossom
Borkovsky, Hershel, 93
Botnick, Joseph, 100
Botnik, Aaron, 101
Bradford Woollens, 128
Braverman, Yankel, 29
Bregman, Henry, 29, 30
Bregman, Mr., of Patricia
  Cloaks, 127
Breslin, Rabbi Yudel
  (Julius) 87
Breslin, Solomon, 89
Brickner, Rabbi Barnet
  A., 74
Brodey & Draimin, 140,
  140*, 142*
Brodey, Zelig, 81
Brody, Abraham, 87
Brody, Moses, 79, 80
Brothers of Jacob, 105
Brown, Bill, 146
Brown, Sam, 29
Brunswick Avenue
  Talmud Torah, 90, 104
Bund, 43, 58, 135
Burke, Jack, 108

- C -

Cahan, Abraham, 35, 43
Canada Linotype Co., 48
Canadian Congress of
  Labour, 138
Canadian Federation of
  Polish Jews, 94
Canadian Jewish
  Congress, 53, 90
Caplan, 13
Caplan, Isadore, 108
Caplan, L., 92
Caplan, Maurice, cantor,
  33
Caplan, Moishe, 33
Cash, Alexander, 103
Cash, Joseph, 121
Cecil Street synagogue
  (Ostrovtzer), 93
Cedarvale, 108-9

Center Palace Hall, 25
Charloff, Berele, cantor,
  99
Chatham, 13
Chevra Bnei Yisroel, 101
Chevra Knesseth Yisroel
  Anshei Slipye, 92
Chevra Shas (Cecil
  Street) 95
Chevra Tehillim, 86
Chomodelsky, Shloime,
  96
Christie Street Talmud
  Torah, 105, 108
Clavir, L., 105
Clavir, Max, 51*, 52, 89
Clavir, M. D. (Moses) 89
Cloakmakers Union, 43,
  119ff
Cohen, Eliezer, 92
Cohen, J., 92
Cohen, M., butcher, 19
Cohen, Mark, 71
Cohen, Mordechai, 92
Cohen, Velvel, 54
Collars & Cuffs Mnfctrs
  Assn., 141
Colofsky, Shimon, 23,
  121
community
  organizations, first
  attempts to establish,
  17
Conan, 14
Congress of Industrial
  Organizations (CIO)
  145
Coombs Drug Store, 69
Christian missionaries,
  27ff

- D -

Dan, Moishe, 35
de Sola, Rabbi Abraham,
  69
Denison, Mary, 146
Dickman, Mordechai,
  first schoichet, 19
Dickstein, Moishe, 49
District Trades and

Labour Council, 143
Donenfeld, B., 92
Dorfman, Mr., 141
Draimin, Charles, 139
Dunkelman, David, 130
Dworkin, Boris, 23
Dworkin, Chanan, 23, 37

- E -

East end Jews, 14
Eaton Co., T., & strike,
  131ff, 131*, 132*, 136
Edell, Pesach, 44*, 78
Eiges, M., 37
Eisen, L., 92
Eisendrath, Rabbi
  Maurice N., 74
Eitz Chaim Talmud
  Torah, 81, 83, 89
Elm Street synagogue,
  see Goel Tzedec
Elzas, Dr. Barnet A., 72
emigrating from Russia,
  16
Englander, A., & Son
  (firm) 140
Englander, Harry, 140
Epstein, Abraham, 37
Ertes, Isaac, 78

- F -

Factor, Judge Samuel, 86
fareinen, 17
Fasser, Sam, 135
Federman, Max, 141,
  143, 146
Federman, N., 92
Feigenbaum, B., 35, 42
Feldheim, Eric, 86
Fidler, Ab. and Feivel
  (brothers) 94
Fineberg, Rabbi
  Abraham, 75
Finkelman, Dr. Jacob,
  123, 138
Finkelstein, Leibish, 34
Finkelstein, Max, 135
First Moldaver

Congregation Tifereth Yisrael Anshei Roumania, 92
Fleishman, Mr., 25
Flich, Louis, 54
Fogel, Moishe, 53
Fogelman, Yitzhak, 53
Folks Farein, 54*
Forcht, S., 108
Forman, Sh., 101
Forum of the Air, 74
Forverts, 37, 40, 42, 43, 57
Foster, Charles, 86
Fox, H. R., 86
Frank, Mr., Hebrew teacher, 107
Frank, M. Z., 53
Frankel, Leo, 19
Frankfort, M., 127
Freifeld, Louis, 139
Friedland, Nathan, 51, 39*, 51*, 52
Frimer, Moishe, 99
Frimes, S, jeweller, 27
Frohlich, S., 82
Frost, Hon. Leslie, 107
fur industry, 139ff
Fur Manufacturers Association, 140
Furriers International Union, 141
Furriers Protective Association, 140

- G -

Gangbar, I., 103
Gar, M., 35
Garfinkel, M., 108
Garfinkle, S.D., 81
Garfunkel, G., 105
Gasner, Meyer W., 108
Gebirtig family, 89
Gebirtig, Mendel, 104
Gelber Brothers, 130
Gelber, Leibish, 79, 80
Gelber, Moses, 79, 82
Gelfand, M., 35
German-Jewish immigrants, 58

Ginsberg & Son, 126
Gitlin, Dr. B., 53
Glantz-Leyeles, Aron, poet, 136
Glass, Mr., 144
Glass, A., 146
Glass, Moishe, 146
Gluck, Rabbi Joseph, 71
Godfrey, Bert, 86
Godfrey, Shloime, 19
Goel Tzedec, 72, 84*, 85ff, 86*
Gold, Ben, 141
Gold, I., 108
Goldberg, Mr. (of Holy Blossom), 69
Goldberg, Mr., printer, 45, 47, 50
Goldenberg, Mr., restaurateur, 24
Goldenberg, A. A., 105
Goldenberg, B. W., 108
Goldenthal, M., 92, 104
Goldman, Emma, 35
Goldsmith, Charles, 9, 10
Goldstein & Jacobs, 127
Golinsky, Sam, 121
Goodman, Rabbi H., 53
Goodman, Moishe, 135
Gordon, Rabbi Jacob, 81*, 85, 88ff, 89*, 104
Gotlieb, Isaac, 94
Gould, 14
Grafstein, Melech, 35
Granatstein, Mendel, 19, 99
Graner Robin Fur Co., 140
Graubart, Rabbi, 83
Green, B., 95
Green, David, 104
Green, I., 103
Green, Marcus, 71
Greenstein, Rabbi V. I., 49
Greisman, 23
Gringorten, Jack, 108
Gringorten, Rabbi, 107
Grouper, Moses, 92
Guillet, E. C., 72, 77
Gurofsky, Joseph, 27
Gurofsky, Louis, 61

- H -

Halpern, Rabbi Isaac, 19, 79, 81
Halpern, P., 53
Hamil, Dr. J. L., 119, 135
Hamilton, 13, 69
Harper, 14
Harris, David, 92
Hart, Arthur D., 9
Hart, Wellington, 68
Hartman, M., 139
Hassidic congregations, 99
Hayman, Lou, 53
Hebrew Benevolent Society, 12
Hebrew Journal, 35*, 39*, 45ff
Hebrew Publishing Co., 48
Heifetz, Solomon, 61
Hellenic Orthodox Church, 74
helping the needy, 60
Henry Street shul, see Beth Jacob
Herman Furs, ad, 142*
Herman, Mr., 130
Herman, Yitzhak, 23, 35
Hershcovitz, Joseph, 92
Hertz, British Chief Rabbi Dr. Joseph H., 109
Hillcrest Congregation, 105-6
Hillman, Sidney, 137-38
Hirsch, H. M., 43ff, 50
Histadrut, 74
History of the Jews in Canada, 9
Holy Blossom, 11, 11*, 12, 30, 69ff, 70*, 73*, 75*, 76*
Hurwich, Kalman, 53
Hurwitz, Yitzhak Isaac, 35
Husatianer Klaus, 83, 99ff, 100
Hutner Brothers, 127

163

- I -

ice cream parlours, 21ff
Imperial Clothing Co., 130
Imperial Tobacco Co., 23
Independent Cloakmkrs Union, 37
Industrial Workers of the World, 119
intelligentsia, 16
International Fur Union, 141
International Handbag Workers Union, 144
International Ladies Garment Workers Union, 37, 111*, 120, 128ff
Isaac, I., 81
Isserman, Rabbi F., 74

- J -

Jacobs, Rabbi Solomon, 30, 73, 88
Jacobson, A., 105, 108
James, Philip (James Brothers Co.) 130
The Jew in Canada, 9
Jewish education, state of, 63
Jewish Express (of London), 30
Jewish Hospital, 59
Jewish Natl. Fund, 103
Jewish World, 52
Johnson, Capt. Fred, 51-2
Joint Board, Cloak, Skirt & Dressmakers Union, 116*
Joseph, Mr. (of Holy Blossom) 69
Joseph, D., 104
Joseph, J. G., 71
Joseph, Simon Alfred, 61
Journal Publications of Toronto, 52
Junction, West Toronto, 90
Just-Rite Cloak Co., 128

- K -

Kalmus, A., cantor, 103
Katz, I. Ch., 101
Katz, S., 146
Kaufman, Morris, 89
Kassel, Max, 71
Kaufman, Mr. (Intl. Fur Union) 141
Kehilath Jacob, 96
Kelman, Rabbi Abraham, 101, 104
Kelman, Rabbi Tsvi, 101
Kennen, J. J., 61
Kerbel, Joseph, 141
Keyfetz, M. H., 105
Kiever congregation, 33, 95-6, 95*
Kimelstein, Dr., 119
King, 14
Kingston, 13, 69
Kirshenbaum, Mr., 141
Kirshenbaum, H. M., 51, 52
Kirzner, Abraham, 116ff, 121, 135
kitchen for unemployed, 32
Kleinman, Mr., 137
Kleppish, Rabbi Zinvil, 97
Kling, O., 105
Knesseth Israel, 90
Kolinum, Sam, 146
Koppel, Mr., teacher, 101
Kosnetaz, Gordon, 54
Kreisman, Dave, 121
Kreisman, Sam, 126
Krochmal, Nachman, 78
Kronick, J., 105
Kronick, Samuel, 123
Kurtz, Abraham, 101
Kurtz, Benjamin, 80, 80*

- L -

Labour Zionists, 35, 57, 66 (See also Poalei Zionists)
Lancaster, Ont., 68
Landman, Rabbi, 72
Landsberg, Mr., 92
landsmanschaften, 17ff, 60, 81ff
Langbord, Maurice, 33
Langer, Chaim, 121
Langner, Rabbi Moishe, 101
Langner, Rabbi Shloime, 101
Lappin, Ben, 53
Lappiner, A., 48
Larenbaum, Abie, 94
Lawson, Hon. Roy, 107
Lazarus, Rabbi Ab., 72
Layefsky, Abraham, 33
Layefsky, Joseph, 33
Leach, Gordon, 146
leather & pocket-book industry, 144
Lederman, Isadore, 146
Lederman, Sam, 146
Leibel, Mr., 130
Lepofsky, J., 108
Lesser, I., 137
Levine, Joseph, 141
Levinson, Yehuda, 103
Leventhal, Harry, 54
Levine, David, 32
Levinter, Shmuel (Samuel) 81, 87, 89
Levy brothers (Hamilton), 68
Levy, Rabbi Meir Zvi, 45
Linson, Abraham, 94
Lipovitz, Aaron, 92
Lister, Marvin, 146
Litvak, Mr. (Kiever) 96
Lubavitch Congregation, 90
Lubelsky, Mr., 130-31, 135
Luftspring, Abraham, 92
Lyons, 14
Lyons, Lewis, 61

- M -

Machzikei Hadat, 82ff, 83*
Magder, Joseph, 92
Maidonick, Mr., 136
Maimon, Berel, 141

Mandel, Albert, 144
Mandelbaum, A. M., 53
Manton Brothers, 48
Margoshes, Dr. S., 53
Markowitz, Mr., 136
Markowitz, Elyahu, 93
Markson, Dr. Charles, 93
Matenko, Isaac, 36*, 135
McCallum, Hiram, mayor, 107
McCaul Street Synagogue, see Beth Hamidrash HaGadol
McKay Street shul, 105
McMillan, Prof., 137
medical dispensary, 27, 60
Megerman, A., 121
Meltchek, Rabbi Meir Yechiel, 97
Menkes, Max, 140
Michaelson's, 24
Miller, Alexander, 71
Miller, Louis, editor, 43
Minkes' Yom Tov Bletter, 37, 40
missing husbands, 61
Mittel, Zalkind, 89
Mizrachi, 90, 92, 107
Monson, Rabbi David, 108, 109*
Morgen Zhurnal, 57
Moscovitz, Joseph, 92
Moses, Mr., printer, 45
Mozirer Sick Benefit Society, 34, 34*, 37

- N -

Nadler, Louis, 108
Naftolin, Gershon, 108
Narayever Congregation, 83, 101
Nashville, Tenn., convention in, 137
Nathanson, Benzion, 104
National Leather Goods, 144
National Radical School (teachers) 36*
National Workers'
Alliance, 43
neutral chairman, 121ff
New York Yiddish dailies, 41
Niagara Falls, 13
Nissenwater, Abraham, 135
Noble, Mr., 130
Nordheimer family, 14, 68-9, 68*, 71
North Bay, 13
Nussbaum, Benzion, 33

- O -

occupations of early immigrants, 59
Ochs, Rabbi Dr. David, 99
Old Folks' Home, 59
One Hundred Years in Toronto (book), 68
Ostrovtzer Synagogue, 25, 93ff, 93*, 94*
Ottawa, 13

- PQ -

Pact, A., 49
Pape Ave. Cemetery, 71
Patricia Cloaks, 127
Pearlman, David, 119
Perl, Joseph, 77
Perlzweig, Rabbi, 85
Phillips, Etta (Lyon) & Nathan, 52
Phillips, Cantor Herman, 72
Poalei Zion, 23, 57, 141
Pocket Workers Union, 145
Poliakov, Saul, 121
Polish Shul, see Beth Jacob
Pollec, L., 89
Poller, Vera, 146
Pomerantz, Joseph, 45
population of Jews in Toronto, 68
Posluns, Louis, 86
Posluns Cloaks & Suits, 127
The Press, 43
Price, A., 127
Price, Rabbi Abraham, 95, 95*
Price, Rabbi Julius, 85
Pride of Israel, 34, 37
Progressive Leather Goods, 144
Pullan, 13
Pullan, Elias, 89
Pullan, J. M., 89
Pullan, M., & Sons, 122*, 127ff

- R -

Rabinovich, Mr., printer, 45, 47, 50
Rabinovitch, Israel, 53
racketeers, 63
Radical School (teachers) 36*
Radomer Hall (Beverley St.) 145
Rappaport, S. I., 77
Reider, S., 89
Rentzer, Ch. L., 92
Renzel, Mr., 130
restaurants, 15*, 24
Rhinewine, Abraham 9, 36*, 39*, 49, 50, 51, 51*, 52, 68, 71
Richmond Street synagogue (Holy Blossom), 71
Rivkin, Sol, 37
Robert Simpson Co., 128
Robinson, Hon. John Beverly, 71
Rodfei Shalom Anshei Kiev, 95
Rodjinsky, Yudel, 121
Rohold, Rev. Sabati, 29ff
Romanick, I. M., 96
Rome, David, 53
Rosen, I, bookkeeper, 23, 49
Rosen, Nathan, 119
Rosenberg, Mr.

165

(manufacturer) 127
Rosenberg, J., 94
Rosenberg, Louis, 9, 49
Rosenberg, Rabbi Yudel, 81*, 83, 96, 97*
Rosenburg, L., 146
Rosenbloom, Mr., 136
Rosenfeld, Jos., 23, 135
Rosenfeld, Morris, poet, 35
Rosenfeld, Samuel, 23, 35, 135
Rosenthal, I., 92
Rosenthal's Drug Stores, 54*
Rosenzweig, M., 95
Ross, Benny, 141
Rotenberg, Louis & Sons, 61, 62*
Rotman, Benny, 121
Rotstein Furniture Co., 54*
Roumanian Jews, 24
Rovner, Abraham, 125, 127, 135
Royal Printing Co., 44*
Rubin, Mr., first baker, 19
ruffians & habitual criminals, 16
Russian-Japanese War, 15

- S -

Sachs, Rabbi Samuel, 85
Sacks, Benjamin 9
St. Clair Robina Hall, 105
St. John's Ward, 12, 13, 14, 40*, 55*, 64*, 77
Saltzman & Son, 126
Salutsky, Mr., of Bund, 135
Samuel & Benjamin (firm) 130
Samuel, W., 108
Samuels, Lewis, 71
Sapirstein, L., 37
Saunders, Mr., 50
Savitzky, Mr., 135
Scheuer, Edmund, 74

Schilds, Rabbi Irwin, 92
Schipper, Frank & Joe, 140
Schipper Freifeld Co., 140
Schon, Bernard, 121
Schulman, Mr., cantor, 88
Schwartz, J. P., Fur Co., 140
Schwartz, Joseph, 140
Schwartz, M., 119
Schwartz, Rabbi Jesse, 85
Schwimmer, Ted, 146
Scott Mission, 32*
Shaarei Shomayim, 105ff, 105*, 106*
Shaarei Tzedec, 92
Shapiro, Ellis I., 86
Shapiro, Rabbi Meir (Lubliner Rav), 99
Shapiro, Rabbi Norman, 85
Shapiro, Shmuel Mayer, 9*, 35, 36*, 47, 49, 50, 51*, 52, 136
Shatz, Charlie, 121
Shatzky, Mr., 130
Shaw Street Shul (Bnai Israel) 101ff, 102*
Shearith Israel, 90
Shemen, N., 53
Sher, Abraham, 47, 50
Shmerler, H., 50
Shochet, Rabbi L., 87
Shomrei Shabbos, 32, 78ff, 92
Shore, Mr., of Beth Sholom, 108
Shore, Max, 135
Shub, Isaac, 80
Shulman, J., 103
Siegel, Mrs. Ida (Lewis) 85
Siegel, Rabbi J. S., 85
Siegel, Moishe, 19, 48
Silverman, Lipe, 93
Silverstein, Kalman, 99
Silverstein, Rabbi Tsvi, 91
Simon brothers, 43
Simon, Harry, 143, 146

Simon, Dr. M. L., 86
Simon, N., 141
Simpson, Robert, Co., 128
Singer, Henry, Rev., 28ff, 31*
Singer, Joshua, 30, 39*, 46
Sivitz, H. M., 61
Skidler Maggid (of London), 30
Skurko, M., 36
Slonim, Rabbi Reuben, 89
Socialist Labour Party, 37, 57
Socialist League, 135
Socialist Territorialists, 37, 57, 66
Solomon, Hershel, 29
Solomon, J., 92
Solway, Mrs., 33
Solway, Dr. J. L., 119
small towns, 13
Spivak, Sol, 136, 138
steamship agents, 61
Stein, Chaim Leib, 100
Stein, David, 135, 146
Stein, Joseph, 136, 137,
Steinberg, Noah, 35
Steinwortzel, Mr., 130
Stone Clothing Co., 130
Strettiner Beth Hamidrash, 83, 101
"summer birds of passage," 120, 127
Sunshine Cloaks, 127
Sussman, C., 52
Sussman, David, 24, 52, 94
Sutton, Mr., 14
Syrkin, Dr. Nachman, 35

- T -

Tageblatt, 37, 40, 42, 43, 57
Tarler Rebbe, see Rosenberg, Rabbi Yudel
Temperance Hall, 85

Teraulay Street synagogue, see Bay Street synagogue
Tifereth Yisrael Anshei Roumania, 92
Tip Top Tailors, 110*, 130
Tobias, Dave, 121
Tobias, I., 92
Torens, General, 69
Toronto Clothing Co., 130
Toronto from Trading Post to Great City, 72, 77
Toronto Hebrew Congregation, see Holy Blossom
Toronto Jewish Kitchen, 33*
Toronto Joint Board, 138
Toronto Kehilla, 89
Toronto Wochenblatt, 43
Tovey, Mr., 136
Traub, S., 86
Tredler, L., 33, 36
Tribune (Yiddish journal), 52
Tucker, Mrs., 24, 33
Turnofsky, M., 103
Tzemach Tzedek (Lubavitch), 90
Tugenhaft, Joseph, 81

- 𝒰𝒱 -

Union of American Hebrew Congreg'ns, 74
United Garment Workers Union, 47, 134, 135ff

University Avenue Synagogue, see Goel Tzedec
Victoria Theatre, 71

- 𝒲 -

Wahrheit, 40, 43, 57
Waksman, Harry, 135
Waldman, Leibele, 107
Wantroff, Adolph, 54
Warshawsky, L., 146
Washer, Rabbi, 107
Wasser, Mordechai, 101
Weber, S., 33
Weinberg, Hillel, 104
Weinberg, Israel, 94
Weinreb, Rabbi Joseph, 78ff, 80*, 81*, 88
Weinstock, Abie, 121
Weisgal, Meyer, 53
Wilder, Chaim, 87
Wilder, Hershel, 33
Wilkowsky, B., 135
Wilson, A., 101
Wilson, Dave, 144
Wilson & Waldman, 127
Winebar, Israel, 141
Wineberg, Harry, 50
Winters & Co., 127
Wittenberg, Rabbi David N., 72
Wladowsky, Bernard, 89
Wochenblatt, 43
Wolfson, Dr., 103
Wolfson, M., 103
Wolinsky, Mr., 121
Workman's Circle, 36-38, 43

Workmen's Circle Peretz School, 36*,

- 𝒳𝒴𝒵 -

Yaffe, Mr., 137
Yampolsky, Mr., 121, 127
Yavneh Zionist congregation, 90, 103
Yehoash, poet, 35, 48
Yeshiva Torah Chayim, 94
Yiddish press, 55ff
Yiddish print shop, 44*
Yiddisher Zhurnal, see *Hebrew Journal*
Yiddish theatre, 24, 35
Yisroel'tche (Rizhiner Rebbe), 100
Young Socialist Club, 35
Zalkin, S., 35
Zalman, Rabbi Schneur, 97
Zeidel, Mr., 130
Zelenko, Louis, 54
Zhitlowsky, Chaim, 35
Zietz, Shloime, 135
Zionist Club (Beverley St.), 37
Zionist Institute, 103
Zisapel, I., 141
Zivitz, see Sivitz
Zucker, Louis, 94, 99

Contact Information

Website
www.nowandthenbookstoronto.com

E-mail
info@nowandthenbookstoronto.com

Postal address
Now and Then Books,
22 Shallmar Blvd., Unit 611,
Toronto, Ont. Canada M5N 2Z8

More titles for you to enjoy from
NOW AND THEN BOOKS

MEMOIRS / LIFE STORIES

¶ I'M NOT GOING BACK: WARTIME MEMOIR OF A CHILD EVACUEE, by Kitty Wintrob. The author recounts the experience of being evacuated as a child from London's Jewish East End to the British countryside at the start of WWII. Great for young readers as well as adults. "The details are absorbing . . . Wintrob gets completely inside her young personality." — *London Jewish Chronicle*. Paperback, 6 x 9 in., 176 pages. $18. (2009)

¶ EIGHTEEN MONTHS: A LOVE STORY INTERRUPTED, by Alan L. Simons. A gripping autobiographical story, moving and inspirational, about the author's relationship with a woman with breast cancer. " . . . a story of devotion, comfort and strength that will touch your heart." Paperback, 5 x 8 in., 116 pages. $18. (2010)

TORONTO / CANADIAN JEWISH HISTORY

¶ ONE HUNDRED YEARS IN CANADA: THE RUBINOFF–NAFTOLIN FAMILY TREE, by Bill Gladstone. Comprehensive genealogical study of a large Toronto-based Jewish family, originally from Belarus, now with branches in many countries. Paperback, 8.25 x 11 in., 384 pages, 700+ photographs, maps & illustrations, plus extensive genealogical charts. Fully indexed. $40. (2008).

¶ THE RISE OF THE TORONTO JEWISH COMMUNITY, by Shmuel Mayer Shapiro. A colourful account to 1950 by the late former editor-publisher of the *Toronto Daily Hebrew Journal*. First edition, with 90 photographs and illustrations; indexed. Paperback, 6 x 9 in., 168 pages. $22. (2010)

¶ THE JEW IN CANADA. Abridged facsimile edition of the classic 1926 volume edited by Arthur D. Hart. Contains all of the biographical and genealogical material of the original edition; only several historical essays have been omitted. Paperback, 8.25 x 11 in. 500+ pages. (*Forthcoming*)

Inquire about our discounts for school, church and reading groups.

www.ingramcontent.com/pod-product-compliance
Lightning Source LLC
Chambersburg PA
CBHW032259150426
43195CB00008BA/505